ROMANTIC IMAGERY IN THE NOVELS
OF CHARLOTTE BRONTË

ROMANTIC IMAGERY IN THE NOVELS OF CHARLOTTE BRONTË

Cynthia A. Linder

BARNES & NOBLE
BOOKS
10 East 53d St., New York 10022
(a division of Harper & Row Publishers, Inc.)

First published 1978 by
THE MACMILLAN PRESS LTD
London and Basingstoke
Published in the U.S.A. 1978 by
HARPER & ROW PUBLISHERS, INC.
BARNES & NOBLE IMPORT DIVISION

Printed in Hong Kong

Library of Congress Cataloging in Publication Data

Linder Cynthia A., 1923
Romantic imagery in the novels of Charlotte Brontë
1.   Brontë, Charlotte, 1816–1855—Styles
2.   Figures of speech
3.   Romanticism—England
I.   Title
PR4169.L5   823'.8   78-2903
ISBN 0-06-494280-5

For Eugenie and Constance

Contents

Acknowledgements

The basis for this study was established during a period of sabbatical leave spent at the University of Exeter, England, and I would like to record my indebtedness to my own university, Rand Afrikaans University, Johannesburg, Republic of South Africa, and, in particular, to the Principal, Professor G. van N. Viljoen, for having granted me the necessary leave to undertake this work. I also wish to acknowledge my appreciation of the financial grant awarded to me by the Human Sciences Research Council of the Republic of South Africa. Furthermore, I wish to thank the members of staff of the Department of English of the University of Exeter for their assistance, and, in particular, my tutor, Mr M. Jones, whose guidance and helpful criticism have been very valuable. Whatever faults this study may have, these are entirely the responsibility of the writer. The library staffs of both universities, as well as of the Brontë Parsonage Museum, have also been unfailing in their assistance in providing background material, and their patience in dealing with my requests is much appreciated. My thanks to the publishers who have allowed me to use material from their published works. Though they are too numerous to list here, their permission has been acknowledged individually in the 'Notes and References' section. Finally, my thanks to a colleague, Dr A. M. Potter, who has carefully read through the text, and pointed out the most obvious errors.

July 1977   C.A.L.

List of Abbreviations

All references to the text of the Brontë novels, and to Mrs Gaskell's *Life of Charlotte Brontë,* have been taken from the Haworth edition of *The Life and Works of Charlotte Brontë and Her Sisters,* edited by Mrs H. Ward and C. K. Shorter, and published in seven volumes by John Murray, 1920.

References to passages in particular novels are indicated by quoting chapter numbers in roman numerals.

The following abbreviations have also been used, with the page number of the cited author.

Allott: Miriam Allott, *The Brontës: The Critical Heritage,* Routledge & Kegan Paul, London, 1974.

BST: *Brontë Society Transactions.*

Gaskell: Mrs E. C. Gaskell, *The Life of Charlotte Brontë,* volume VII of the Haworth edition.

Gérin: Dr W. Gérin, *Charlotte Brontë: The Evolution of Genius,* Oxford University Press, 1967. (By permission of the Oxford University Press.)

PMLA: Publications of the Modern Language Association of America.

Shorter: C. K Shorter, *The Brontës and Their Circle,* J. M. Dent, 1914.

I   The Evolution of Form

Charlotte Brontë's novels present a problem for the critic who is
concerned with the study of narrative patterns, as there appears to
be only a very superficial similarity between the four novels she
wrote for publication, *The Professor, Jane Eyre, Shirley* and *Villette*.
Three are written in an autobiographical form, whilst the fourth,
Shirley, is a chronicle of society set in historical time, and narrated
by the omniscient and present author, who observes and comments
on character, action and event. Furthermore, in two of the three
novels written in the autobiographical form, there are 'gothicisms'
which seem to be extrinsic to the main story. In *Jane Eyre* there is
the description of the mysterious third floor at Thornfield, the
suspicious behaviour of Grace Poole, screams, and the inexplicable
accidents that take place in Rochester's bedroom, while in *Villette*,
there is the apparition of a nun who flits through the garden and
attic room of the Pensionnat de Demoiselles, but Charlotte Brontë
has not made use of the non-rational elements in her third autobiographical novel, *The Professor*. This is the first problem the
critic has to solve – is the supernatural material extrinsic or intrinsic to the work as a whole; is it included for the excitement of the
reader, in which case it is extrinsic to the main purpose of the novel,
or does it advance the plot, explain the character and background?
If it does, then it is intrinsic. That this is an important critical point
can be seen in a reading of contemporary nineteenth-century criticism, which judges *Shirley* to be inferior to the other two novels,
on the grounds that 'It does not so rivet the reader's attention, nor
hurry him through all obstacles of improbability, with so keen a
sympathy in [its] reality'. (Allott: 163). It is G. H. Lewes who has
made this observation, but he is expressing a view held by other
critics as well, that the lack of inventiveness in depicting incident is
a weakness in *The Professor* and *Shirley*. In fact, on this criterion,
Jane Eyre and *Villette* are given first place, whilst *Shirley* is given
an honourable mention, and *The Professor* is ignored.

To criticise a work because the narrative technique differs from
another work by the same author seems to me to be unjustified, unless the author has not fulfilled the claims she has stated, but this
can only be established after a study of the author's claims, in this
instance presented in Prefaces and correspondence. From a study of
the Miriam Allott collection of criticism, it is obvious that the
absence of a thorough examination of Charlotte Brontë's own
statements on her work has affected the quality of Brontë criticism.
However, there is a large quantity of background material available
to the critic, contained in the T. J. Wise four-volume collection of

her letters, the Clement Shorter two-volume edition of her letters, and in Mrs E. C. Gaskell's biography. This source material provides information on Charlotte Brontë's correspondence to her friends Ellen Nussey, Mary Taylor and Miss Wooler, to her publisher George Smith, to his reader W. S. Williams, and to the critic G. H. Lewes, and gives the reader a picture of Charlotte Brontë's personality, in presenting her opinions on life, love, family ties, religion and writing. In the course of my study of the individual novels I shall refer to Mrs Gaskell's biography, and to Charlotte's letters to W. S. Williams, indicating the use of autobiographical material, when and where this information is useful for a better understanding of the writer's intentions and successes. For the present I wish only to present, in the form of a dialogue, an exchange of ideas on the 'art' of writing between Charlotte Brontë and G. H. Lewes, because this will clearly demonstrate my contention that Charlotte Brontë shows an awareness of the 'art' of writing, which Lewes does not always recognise. I have chosen Lewes because he is the only contemporary critic with whom Charlotte Brontë corresponded, and who had written reviews on three of her four novels, only omitting to write a review on *The Professor,* which was published posthumously, in 1857. The correspondence began in 1847; after Lewes had read *Jane Eyre* he wrote to her saying how delighted he had been by the quality of this work from an unknown author, but suggested that for future novels she should restrict herself to the depiction of real experience. Charlotte Brontë's reply to Lewes is illuminating in that it is, firstly, a statement of principles on the craft of writing, secondly, it gives some background information as to why *The Professor* was not accepted for publication, and thirdly, it explains the origin of the melodramatic elements in *Jane Eyre*. She states (Gaskell: 343):

You warn me to beware of melodrama, and you exhort me to adhere to the real. When I first began to write, so impressed was I with the truth of the principles you advocate, that I determined to take Nature and Truth as my sole guides, and to follow to their very footprints; I restrained imagination, eschewed romance, repressed excitement; over-bright colouring, too, I avoided, and sought to produce something which should be soft, grave, and true.

My work (a tale in one volume) being completed, I offered it to a publisher. He said it was original, faithful to nature, but he did not feel warranted in accepting it; such a work would not sell. I tried six publishers in succession; they all told me it was deficient in 'startling incident' and 'thrilling excitement', that it would never suit the circulating libraries, and as it was on those libraries the success of works of fiction mainly depended, they could not undertake to publish what would be overlooked there.

As Charlotte Brontë was determined to earn her livelihood through her writing, it is not surprising that she took care in her second novel, *Jane Eyre,* to provide her readers with the 'startling incident' and 'thrilling excitement' that *The Professor* seemed to lack. The question remains, was she successful in fusing the 'gothic' elements with the main narrative? Apparently not, as Lewes, in his review of *Jane Eyre,* published in *Fraser's Magazine,* states that (Allott: 85):

There are some defects in it – defects which the excellence of the rest only brings into stronger relief. There is, indeed, too much melodrama and improbability, which smack of the circulating-library, – we allude particularly to the mad wife and all that relates to her, and to the wanderings of Jane when she quits Thornfield; yet even those parts are powerfully executed. But the earlier parts – all those relating to Jane's childhood and her residence at Lowood, with much of the strange love story – are written with remarkable beauty and truth. The characters are few, and drawn with unusual mastery: even those that are but sketched – such as Mr Brocklehurst, Miss Temple, Mrs Fairfax, Rosamund, and Blanche – are sketched with a vividness which betrays the cunning hand: a few strokes, and the figure rises before you. Jane herself is a creation. The delicate handling of this figure alone implies a dramatic genius of no common order. We never lose sight of her plainness; no effort is made to throw romance about her – no extraordinary goodness or cleverness appears to your admiration; but you admire, you love her, – love her for the strong will, honest mind, loving heart, and peculiar but fascinating person.

Lewes comments favourably on Charlotte Brontë's ability in the art of verbal portraiture, but omits any reference to, or discussion of, narrative techniques in *Jane Eyre*. It is known that Charlotte read the review, as shortly after its publication she wrote to Lewes stating that (Gaskell: 351):

I mean to observe your warning about being careful how I undertake new works. My stock of materials is not abundant, but very slender; and, besides, neither my experience, my acquirements, nor my powers are sufficiently varied to justify my ever becoming a frequent writer . . . .
If I ever *do* write another book, I think I will have nothing of

what you call 'melodrama'; I *think* so, but I am not sure. I *think*, too, I will endeavour to follow the counsel which shines out of Miss Austen's 'mild eyes', 'to finish more and be more subdued'; but neither am I sure of that. When authors write best, or, at least, when they write most fluently, an influence seems to waken in them, which becomes their master – which will have its own way – putting out of view all behests but its own, dictating certain words, and insisting on their being used, whether vehement or measured in their nature; new-moulding characters, giving unthought-of turns to incidents, rejecting carefully elaborated old ideas, and suddenly creating and adopting new ones.

Two years after having written to Lewes about the influences which determined her style of narrative form, Charlotte Brontë published her second novel, *Shirley,* which Lewes reviewed for the *Edinburgh Review,* stating that in his opinion (Allott: 163-4):

Shirley is inferior to *Jane Eyre* in several important points. It is not quite so true; and it is not so fascinating. It does not so rivet the reader's attention, nor hurry him through all obstacles of improbability, with so keen a sympathy in its reality. It is even coarses in texture, too, and not unfrequently flippant; while the characters are almost all disagreeable, and exhibit intolerable rudeness of manner. In *Jane Eyre* life was viewed from the standing point of individual experience; in *Shirley* that standing point is frequently abandoned, and the artist paints only a panorama of which she, as well as you, are but spectators. Hence the unity of *Jane Eyre* in spite of its clumsy and improbable contrivances, was great and effective: the fire of one passion fused the discordant materials into one mould. But in *Shirley* all unity, in consequence of defective art, is wanting. There is no passionate link; nor is there any artistic fusion, or intergrowth, by which one part evolves itself from another. Hence its falling-off in interest, coherent movement, and life. The book may be laid down at any chapter, and almost any chapter might be omitted.

That this review hurt Charlotte Brontë is not surprising, nor is it unexpected that in her next novel, *Villette,* she returned to the narrative form of the successful *Jane Eyre.* This is not the place for a discussion of Lewes' point of view, the validity or opaqueness of which will, I hope, be made apparent in my analysis of *Shirley,* in Chapter 4, but it is important to know that Charlotte Brontë wrote to Lewes about this review, taxing him for distinguishing female writers from the *genus* author, believing, quite rightly, that the merit of a novel should be determined exclusively by the evidence

contained within the work itself. (Gaskell: 438-9). *Villette* was
published at the end of January 1853, and two weeks later there
appeared an unsigned review in the *Leader*, which had, in fact,
been written by Lewes; his verdict on *Villette* being that (Allott:
185):

> . . . considered in the light of a novel, it is a less interesting story
> than even *Shirley*. It wants the unity and progression of interest
> which made *Jane Eyre* so fascinating; but it is the book of a mind
> more conscious of its power.

There is no record of Charlotte Brontë being aware who the
reviewer was, nor how she judged this article, but that she was
concerned about the opinion of critics on her work, the following
extract from a letter she wrote to W. S. Williams shows. She states
(Gaskell: 605):

> Were a review to appear, inspired with treble their animus, *pray*
> do not withhold it from me. I like to see the satisfactory notices
> – especially I like to carry them to my father – but I *must* see
> such as are *un*satisfactory and hostile; these are for my own
> especial edification; it is in these I best read public feeling and
> opinion. To shun examination into the dangerous and disagree-
> able seems to me cowardly. I long always to know what really *is*,
> and am only unnerved when kept in the dark. . . .
> As to the character of 'Lucy Snowe', my intention from the first
> was that she should not occupy the pedestal to which 'Jane Eyre'
> was raised by some injudicious admirers. She is where I meant her
> to be, and where no charge of self-laudation can touch her.

The foregoing dialogue between Lewes and Charlotte Brontë has
clarified the problem of the changes in structure to be found in her
four novels. Charlotte Brontë wrote *Shirley* in that form, because
she thought that was what the public wanted, taking Lewes' opinion as a barometer of public taste. But it does not answer the second
problem, whether Lewes was correct in his statement that there are
defects of unity in *Jane Eyre*, *Shirley* and *Villette*. It is my intention
in the following chapters to study each of the novels independently,
by tracing the pattern of the narrative through the predominating
imagery used in that novel, and to consider whether that imagery,
be it artefacts of civilisation, or taken from nature, is an effective
means of conveying simultaneously both subjective and objective
levels of meaning. Expressing the problem in twentieth-century
critical terminology – are the chosen 'objective correlatives' successful in their designated function of presenting states of mind and

feeling, and an appropriate symbolisation of the situation of the character in question, at any particular place in the narrative? Finally, I hope, in the course of my examination, to determine whether the melodramatic elements in *Jane Eyre* and *Villette* have been successfully fused into the novel, so that they become an intrinsic part of the structure of that novel. It is only after such a study has been undertaken that one is in a position to comment on the quality of Charlotte Brontë's artistic ability, and my findings, after a close study of each of the novels, will be given in the Conclusion.

2   *The Professor*

Charlotte Brontë wrote *The Professor* in the form of an autobiography, using the central character, William Crimsworth, as the narrator of events. The novel begins with a description of his experiences as a young man in England, his adult life in Brussels, and finally, his life of retirement when he returns to England with his wife and son. Variety is given to the linear pattern by dividing the novel into three geographical sections, which correspond to differing stages of Crimsworth's material and emotional development, all of which are held together by a strict chronological order, but from the point of view of an elderly man. Thus, the structure of the novel is a simple and straightforward chronological exposition of events beginning in Chapter II. Chapter I is a rather clumsy presentation of some background information, which could have been omitted, and the facts incorporated in Chapter II, as it is written in the form of a letter to an old school friend named Charles, whom we do not hear of again.

The story proper begins in Chapter II, when William Crimsworth goes to the north of England to stay with his brother and sister-in-law, hoping to be given some employment by his brother, who is a wealthy mill-owner. The brother, Edward Crimsworth, offers him a post as clerk at the factory, but tells William that he is not to expect any marks of favouritism. On the contrary, Edward seems to resent his brother's superior education, as his education at Eton had been paid for by two uncles, and is pointedly rude, even hostile, to William on every occasion that they meet. The work of translating foreign correspondence that William is given to do is extremely dull, and he is not sorry when he is dismissed by Edward on the pretext that he has spread malicious gossip about him around the town. Although William is glad to end this servile work, he is afraid of the future, as he has no money, qualifications, or friends. At this point, an acquaintance, Mr Hunsden, who is, by nature, a very brusque character, suggests to William that he should go abroad and try to earn his livelihood there, and gives him an introduction to a friend living in Brussels. William's decision to go to Brussels concludes the first section of the novel; he is 21 years of age.

The second section begins with William's journey to Brussels, depicts his arrival there, and describes how he obtains a post as a teacher at a boys' school, with the help of Hunsden's letter of introduction. The Brussels section forms the major part of the novel, and in it we are given a picture of William's mental and emotional growth. The reader is given an account of his experiences as a teacher at the boys' school, which is directed by a M. Pelet, and his infatuation with Mlle Reuter, the directress of a neighbouring girls' school, from which he extricates himself when he learns that she is secretly engaged to M. Pelet, and, finally, his meeting with, falling in love, and marriage to Mlle Henri, who is his pupil. This section ends with a portrayal of his married life. He is now middle-aged, is the successful head of a boys' school, and the father of a boy named Victor. The final section of the novel gives an account of the Crimsworths' return to England, which they are enabled to do through having worked hard, lived frugally, and having saved enough money to live comfortably in their retirement.

It is a story without any excitement, but it is what Charlotte Brontë wanted to write, and she consciously and rigidly controlled the language and situation to present a picture of life in the middling stage of success. The fact that she chose such a prosaic setting of hard endeavour to present the life of her hero may seem strange to the readers of her Angrian stories, where flamboyant characters are constantly shown in exotic countries facing superhuman challenges, but it was her stated aim to control her imagination, and check extravagance in the first novel which she wrote for publication. In the Preface to the novel, Charlotte Brontë states the principle underlying the writing of the novel was that:

> . . . my hero should work his way through life as I had seen real living men work theirs – that he should never get a shilling he had not earned – that no sudden turns should lift him in a moment to wealth and high station; that whatever small competency he might gain, should be won by the sweat of his brow; that, before he could find so much as an arbour to sit down in, he should master at least half the ascent of 'the Hill of Difficulty'; that he should not even marry a beautiful girl or lady of rank. As Adam's son he should share Adam's doom, and drain throughout life a mixed and moderate cup of enjoyment.

It is a fact that the picture of William's climb up the 'Hill of Difficulty' is a sombre one, painted predominantly in dark colours, in which is depicted his struggle for economic independence and a fulfilled emotional life. The language reflects the mood of the narrator, which is serious and restrained, with few excursions into the poetic or extravagant, and with no exciting incidents to relieve the grey picture of a 'mixed and moderate cup of enjoyment'. Even William's visit to Mlle Henri, when he proposes marriage to her, is described in restrained language, and painted in subdued colouring, as the following extract shows (XXIII):

I came forward, bade Frances 'good evening', and took my seat.

The chair I had chosen was one she had probably just left; it stood by a little table where were her open desk and papers. I know not whether she had fully recognized me at first, but she did so now; and in a voice, soft but quiet, she returned my greeting. I had shown no eagerness; she took her cue from me, and evinced no surprise. We met as we had always met, as master and pupil – nothing more. I proceeded to handle the papers; Frances observant and serviceable, stepped into an inner room, brought a candle, lit it, placed it by me; then drew the curtain over the lattice, and having added a little fresh fuel to the already bright fire, she drew a second chair to the table, and sat down at my right hand, a little removed.

The restraint of the feeling is reflected in the quietness of William's entry into the room, his subdued greeting, and the statement that their relationship was that of master and pupil. The only light in the picture is that of the candle, and the only warmth that given off by the bright fire. This is not a bright illumination of an important episode in William's life, more appropriate, in fact, as an illustration of the domesticity of a long-married couple. Indeed, Charlotte Brontë makes it absolutely clear that the William Crimsworth – Mlle Henri marriage is not to be a flight from reality into a world of sunshine and sensuality, but a partnership in which both persons through their endeavour and perseverance establish for themselves a niche in the prosaic world of labour. It is Mlle Henri's capacity for hard work and self-restraint which attracts William to her, as he says (XIX):

I loved the movement with which she confided her hand to my hand; I loved her as she stood there, penniless and parentless; for a sensualist charmless, for me a treasure – my best object of sympathy on earth, thinking such thoughts as I thought, feeling such feelings as I felt; my ideal of the shrine in which to seal my stores of love; personification of discretion and forethought, of diligence and perseverance, and self-denial and self-control – those guardians, those trusty keepers of the gift I longed to confer on her – the gift of all my affections; model of truth and honour, of independence and conscientiousness – those refiners and sustainers of an honest life; silent possessor of a well of tenderness, of a flame, as genial as still, as pure as quenchless, of natural feeling, natural passion – those sources of refreshment and comfort to the sanctuary of home.

This passage is a fair representation of the general tone of the novel, in which puritanical attitudes are blended with Romantic method, so that the love portrayed is practical rather than sensual, and it is consistent with the change of style that Charlotte Brontë has chosen, as she relates, in the Preface, that she 'had got over any such taste as I might once have had for ornamented and redundant composition', and it is a fact that there are no implausible occurrences, or improbable characters to assist the hero up the 'Hill of Difficulty'. The only events which do not arise from William's endeavours are those initiated by Mr Hunsden, and they are of a practical nature in keeping with the theme and character portrayal in the novel. Apart from the letter of introduction to a Mr Brown, which has already been noted, Hunsden also sends William the portrait of his mother, which he had bought when Edward's household effects are auctioned due to the latter's failure in business.

Hunsden's presence is necessary in the novel, as he functions as the goad which prods William to act, and his optimism and energy are a foil to William's natural tendency to mental and physical inertia, and, on occasion, to his despondency. The effect of Hunsden on William can be seen in the 'picture' episode, which would seem to be superfluous, unless it were interpreted in the light of evidence obtained from the first passage in which the painting is mentioned. The reference to the painting occurs in the scene in which William describes his first dinner party at his brother's house, when he meets his sister-in-law for the first time. The description of the sister-in-law, with her garish appearance of red hair, bright eyes, and a round face, is contrasted with the picture of William's mother, who has a thoughtful expression, and serious eyes. Although William has no experience of women, his instinctive reaction is one of approval for the type represented by his mother, and distaste for the flamboyancy of his sister-in-law. Nevertheless, when he arrives in Brussels, and meets Mlle Reuter, he is attracted to her, despite the great similarity between Mlle Reuter and his sister-in-law; the attraction to the latter person being her foreign quality and her physicality. This last he finds most disturbing, so much so that even when he knows that she is about to marry M. Pelet he is still excited by her, as he says (XX):

I was no pope – I could not boast infallibility: in short, if I stayed, the probability was that, in three months' time, a practical modern French novel would be in full process of concoction under the roof of the unsuspecting Pelet. Now, modern French novels are not to my taste, either practically or theoretically. Limited as had yet been my experience of life, I had once had the opportunity of contemplating, near at hand, an example of the results produced by a course of interesting and romantic domestic treachery.

As William does not intend to play the part of villain in the
Pelet household, he resigns his post, an act which is in keeping with
the rôle Charlotte Brontë had envisaged for him. It is at this point
that Hunsden appears in his life again. Crimsworth tries to evade
Hunsden's more probing questions, as he knows that it is 'not easy
to blind Hunsden'. Evidently not, for the morning after this conversation, Hunsden has the picture delivered to William's room,
using it as a visual exemplum to remind him of his natural affinity
to purity and simplicity, and, by implication, the portrait suggests
that Mlle Reuter is the antithesis of this, whereas William would
be able to recognise the similarity existing between his mother and
Mlle Henri. The picture, then, crystallises what William instinctively knows, but has not allowed himself to acknowledge, that though
he may harbour feelings of sensuality, nevertheless his 'road' leads
in a different direction. Subsequent to the receipt of this gift, William is goaded into action, he visits Vandenhuten in the hope of
getting employment, and, when he has obtained this, he visits Mlle
Henri. Thus, the novel shows evidence of the 'art' being more
subtle than a superficial reading would indicate, and it shows,
furthermore, that Charlotte Brontë was able to 'see' objectively the
total character, and to create situations in which aspects of personality are dramatically portrayed.

A particularly interesting example of the adoption of material
from Charlotte Brontë's own life to that of her hero's is the trans-
formation of the matter of a letter Charlotte had received from
Southey into a statement of Mlle Reuter's to William about Mlle
Henri's literary aspirations, and his conduct towards her; she says
(XVIII):

> . . . the sentiment of *amour-propre* has a somewhat marked pre-
> ponderance in her character; celebrity has a tendency to foster
> this sentiment, and in her it should be rather repressed – she
> rather needs keeping down than bringing forward; and then I
> think, Monsieur – is appears to me that ambition, *literary* ambi-
> tion especially, is not a feeling to be cherished in the mind of a
> woman: would not Mlle Henri be much safer and happier if
> taught to believe that in the quiet discharge of social duties con-
> sists her real vocation, than if stimulated to aspire after applause
> and publicity? She may never marry; scanty as are her resources,
> obscure as are her connections, uncertain as is her health (for I
> think her consumptive, her mother died of that complaint), it is
> more than probable she never will: I do not see how she can rise
> to a position whence such a step would be possible; but even in
> celibacy it would be better for her to retain the character and
> habits of a respectable decorous female.

The tone of this passage, and the sentiment expressed by Mlle Reuter, is entirely in keeping with her other observations on life; it is a true reflection of the thoughts and feelings of the particular character that Charlotte Brontë is delineating, and yet it is also a true reflection of the tenor of Southey's letter to Charlotte, which he wrote when he returned some verses to her. His letter reads (Gaskell: 156):

But it is not with a view to distinction that you should cultivate this talent, if you consult your own happiness. I, who have made literature my profession, and devoted my life to it, and have never for a moment repented of the deliberate choice, think myself nevertheless, bound in duty to caution every young man who applies as an aspirant to me for encouragement and advice against taking so perilous a course. You will say that a woman has no need of such a caution; there can be no peril in it for her. In a certain sense this is true; but there is a danger of which I would, with all kindness and all earnestness, warn you. The day dreams in which you habitually indulge are likely to induce a distempered state of mind; and, in proportion as all the ordinary uses of the world seem to you flat and unprofitable, you will be unfitted for them without becoming fitted for anything else. Literature cannot be the business of a woman's life, and it ought not to be. The more she is engaged in her proper duties, the less leisure will she have for it, even as an accomplishment and a recreation. To those duties you have not yet been called, and when you are you will be less eager for celebrity. You will not seek in imagination for excitement, of which the vicissitudes of this life, and the anxieties from which you must not hope to be exempted, be your state what it may, will bring with them but too much.

In a comparison of these two passages it is obvious that Mlle Reuter has the same antipathetic attitude as Southey towards women writers, thus when one considers the personality of the echo, one can infer what Charlotte Brontë thought of Southey's advice. Nevertheless, it provided her with material for a marvellously satiric sketch of Mlle Reuter, and it adequately disposed of Southey's advice.

There is, however, one aspect of Charlotte Brontë's personality which many readers of *The Professor* do not think that she has managed to graft successfully onto her chosen protagonist in the novel. It is the passage where William, after having proposed to, and been accepted by, Mlle Henri, returns to his room and experiences a period of extreme dejection, in which he hears a voice saying

'In the midst of life we are in death', and goes on to explain this experience (XXIII):

> That sound, and the sensation of chill anguish accompanying it, many would have regarded as supernatural; but I recognised it at once as the effect of reaction. Man is ever clogged with his mortality, and it was my mortal nature which now faltered and plained; my nerves, which jarred and gave a false sound, because the soul, of late rushing headlong to an aim, had overstrained the body's comparative weakness. A horror of great darkness fell upon me; I felt my chamber invaded by one I had known formerly, but had thought for ever departed. I was temporarily a prey to hypochondria.

It is true that William has recently been active in trying to find other employment, after his resignation from M. Pelet's school, but this activity, and his decision to ask Mlle Henri to marry him seems hardly a justification for hypochondria, and his situation is by no means comparable to the situations which gave rise to Miss Brontë's periods of hypochondria. In this respect, Lucy Snowe's fit of depression, when she is forced to stay with the cretin, is entirely probable considering the nature of the person and the situation in which she is placed. Thus, in *The Professor,* Miss Brontë has not adapted this autobiographical material so that it would seem to be an entirely natural attitude of the character responding to a situation, though she did succeed in *Villette.* On the other hand, it must be stated that Charlotte Brontë places this passage on hypochondria between two passages which provide the reader with some rather interesting information on William's personality, which the reader could have inferred from certain of his previous actions and statements, but which Charlotte Brontë purposefully keeps obscure – the inherent sensuality of her hero. In the first passage William relates his surprise when he discovered that (XXIII):

> I derived a pleasure, purely material, from contemplating the clearness of her brown eyes, the fairness of her fine skin, the purity of her well-set teeth, the proportion of her delicate form; and that pleasure I could ill have dispensed with. It appeared, then, that I too was a sensualist, in my temperate and fastidious way.

It is obvious that an attractive female form has a strong effect on his emotions. The second passage follows on the description of the hypochondriacal attack, which William relates he has experienced before during his adolescence, but which was then justified because:

. . . my boyhood was lonely, parentless; uncheered by brother or sister; and there was no marvel that, just as I rose to youth, a sorceress, finding me lost in vague mental wanderings, with many affections and few objects, glowing aspirations and gloomy prospects, strong desires and slender hopes, should lift up her illusive lamp to me in the distance, and lure me to her vaulted home of horrors. No wonder her spells *then* had power; but *now* . . . why did hypochondria accost me now?

The answer to William's question is connected with his previous feelings of nascent sexuality, as an adolescent, and with his present realisation that Mlle Frances Henri is not plain-looking, which has evoked a similar physical and emotional response. In fact, what Charlotte Brontë is trying to say is that William is responding in an adolescent physical way to Mlle Henri. In this passage, then, Charlotte Brontë comes as close to stating as Victorian propriety will allow, that William's attack of morbidity is the result of suppressed sexuality. However, it is difficult to prove this interpretation, as the language is vague rather than veiled: This is understandable when one recalls some of the animadversions to *Jane Eyre,* which Charlotte Brontë might well have had in mind when rereading the script of, and writing the Preface to, *The Professor,* in 1849.

It cannot be denied that the basic materials from which *The Professor* is constructed are experiences taken from the author's own life. Charlotte Brontë was a student in Brussels for two years, from 1842 to 1843, having decided, at the age of 26, that she needed to have better qualifications if she and her sister Emily were to proceed with their plan of opening a girls' school, in Yorkshire. In her second year at the Pensionnat Héger Charlotte was offered the post of pupil-teacher, at a salary of £16 per annum, which would enable her to pay for the lessons she was still receiving. This work she accepted, and there is no doubt that the descriptions of the life of a teacher that are recounted by William Crimsworth, in *The Professor,* and the portraits of the various pupils whom he has to teach, are drawn from recollections of experiences that Charlotte had while she was in Brussels. This can be proved by a comparison of the amount of information that William gives us about the boys' school with the detailed information that he gives us about his female pupils. There is only one description of a lesson at M. Pelet's school, the one William gave in order to prove his competency as a teacher to M. Pelet, and in that episode the personalities of his pupils are described in only very general terms, The boy who is asked to read from *The Vicar of Wakefield* is described as a 'moon-faced young Flamand in a blouse' named Jules, whose efforts with a strange language are criticised by William, who recalls that (VII):

. . . it might, however, have been a Runic scroll for any resemblance the words, as enunciated by Jules, bore to the language in ordinary use amongst the natives of Great Britain. My God! how he did snuffle, snort, and wheeze! All he said was said in the throat and nose, for it is thus the Flamands speak, but I heard him to the end of his paragraph without proffering a word of correction, whereat he looked vastly self-complacent, convinced, no doubt, that he had acquitted himself like a real born and bred 'Anglais'. In the same unmoved silence I listened to a dozen in rotation, and when the twelfth had concluded with splutter, hiss, and mumble, I solemnly laid down the book.

It is evident, from the content of this passage, that William's opinions on the poor pronunciation of his Belgian pupils could equally be applied to girls – there is no distinctive male quality described in his pupils, whereas, when Crimsworth is appointed as a teacher of English at Mlle Reuter's school, we are given detailed descriptions of some of his pupils (X):

Eulalie was tall, and very finely shaped: she was fair, and her features were those of a Low Country Madonna; many a 'figure de Vierge' have I seen in Dutch pictures exactly resembling hers; there were no angles in her shape or in her face, all was curve and roundness – neither thought, sentiment, nor passion disturbed by line or flush the equality of her pale, clear skin; her noble bust heaved with her regular breathing, her eyes moved a little – by these evidences of life alone could I have distinguished her from some large handsome figure moulded in wax. Hortense was of middle size and stout, her form ungraceful, her face striking, more alive and brilliant than Eulalie's, her hair was dark brown, her complexion richly coloured; there were frolic and mischief in her eye: consistency and good sense she might possess, but none of her features betokened those qualities.

The chapter continues with a description of the sensual Caroline, and the ugly, but clever and hard-working, Sylvie. Thus, from a comparison of the two passages, it is clear that the description of the boys is in general terms, whilst that of the girls is specific, detailed, and with particular characters in mind. This suggests that the author knew the female scholar better than she knew the male, but it also indicates a movement in the novel from the theme of material security, which has been the central concern of William up to this point, to the theme of emotional awakening, which begins with his entry into Mlle Reuter's school. William's emotional vulnerability is implied in the following passage (X):

> I carefully and deliberately made these observations before allow-
> ing myself to take one glance at the benches before me; having
> handled the crayon, looked back at the tableau, fingered the
> sponge in order to ascertain that it was in the right state of
> moisture, I found myself cool enough to admit of looking calmly
> up and gazing deliberately round me.

A little further on he tells us that he did 'not bear the first view
like a stoic'. This detailed description of a slow and controlled
entry into the teaching situation could only have been written by
someone who has had such an experience, but the experience is
reworked here so that it becomes a description which is entirely
consistent with the character at this point in the novel, and suggestive of certain propensities in William's character, which will be
developed later in the novel. In fact, from the point in the novel
where William enters into the life of Mlle Reuter's establishment
his main concern is with affairs of the heart, although this change
is not shown in an alteration in the language, which continues in
the same controlled expository form found in the earlier part of
the novel.

It is obvious that, though the novels are based on experiences
which took place in the life of the author, these experiences have
not been subjectively transposed to the novels; on the contrary, a
very important transforming process has taken place, in which the
mind of the writer has objectively reworked her own experiences,
and presented them as originating in the life of her character. It is
true that the subject matter of Charlotte Brontë's novels is mainly
centred around governesses, schools, and the endeavour to obtain
economic independence, subjects which were of great concern and
interest to her personally, but, in the novels, they become the
problems of the character and not of the author. That this is so,
has, I believe, been demonstrated in the transformation of the content of the Southey letter, so that, in the novel, it becomes a perfectly assimilated and probable expression of the character who is
speaking. Another similar reworking by Charlotte of her experience
at the Pensionnat Héger is the detailed description of the girls'
class in the pensionnat of Mlle Reuter, which has a metaphoric
value in depicting the development of William Crimsworth's character and career, and there are other instances in the novel showing
a similar kind of authorial control over her own experience, such
as William's visit to the graveyard where he meets Mlle Henri,
which is based on a visit of Charlotte to the grave of Martha Taylor, at Brussels. To hunt the Brontë biographies and letters for an
explication of the texts of the novels is to ignore the creative talent
of the writer, and, in many instances, it leads to an incorrect inter-

pretation of the text.

From the evidence that has already been presented, it would appear that Charlotte Brontë's mind was consciously engaged on the creation of a work of art, and that her artistic vision saw the character in a particular situation completely objectively, and, through a process of imaginative projection, by distancing herself from the character and event she was describing, she was able to make use of her own experiences; this suggests that she was applying to her mature writing qualities of discrimination and judgement. An interesting observation that William makes with regard to the work that Mlle Henri executes for him distinguishes between her earlier efforts in writing and her later endeavours, the difference being between qualities of fancy and taste in the earlier work, and judgement and imagination in her later writing. He says (XVIII):

> Such occupation seemed the very breath of her nostrils, and soon her improved productions wrung from me the avowal that those qualities in her I had termed taste and fancy ought rather to have been denominated judgement and imagination.

This statement follows another comment where he speaks about her exercise on King Alfred (XVI):

> As to the substance of your devoir Mlle Henri, it has surprised me; I perused it with pleasure, because I saw in it some proofs of taste and fancy.

It would seem, therefore, that Charlotte Brontë was herself aware that her Juvenilia writings are the product of 'taste' and 'fancy', but that she subdued 'fancy' and used her powers of imagination and judgement when creating her novels.

The creative power of her imagination in the mature novels can, I think, be observed in her selection and use of imagery to portray the state of mind and feeling of a character, which would be difficult to express descriptively. It will be shown that in all her novels references to literature are used in the form of similes or metaphors for character portrayal, and that nature imagery is used as an 'objective correlative' to portray states of mind or feeling. The latter is a particularly Romantic mode whereby the writer, in order to define a mood, takes a symbol from nature to illustrate visually what would otherwise require a lengthy description. By far the most distinctive quality of Charlotte Brontë's narrative technique is the choice of a setting for her characters. It is as if she 'saw' them in a particular place concerned with a particular experience, and their placing in relation to a focal point in the picture determines their position in the situation. The eye that sees the character is objective, but the details surrounding the character are drawn in an impressionistic style, so that there is a double perspective, that of the writer towards her subject matter, and the character towards his situation. Thus, angle of vision serves a double function, as it illustrates what the character is thinking, and it also illustrates the limitation of vision that the character has at a particular point in the narrative. In *The Professor* Charlotte Brontë makes use of certain recurring symbols and metaphors, used consistently throughout the novel, to show the changes that are taking place in her hero's personality. These changes in feeling are shown through his attitude and position to the symbols of the fireside, sky and nature, and gardens. Furthermore, literary references are occasionally employed as similes to define the attitude or thought of a particular character to other characters or events.

There are twenty-two references to the 'fireside', which Charlotte Brontë uses to signify moments and events of importance taking place in Crimsworth's life, and which symbolise William's feelings at that stage of his career. The first reference to a fireside occurs when William visits his brother's house, where he is ushered 'into a room furnished as a library, where there was a bright fire, and candles burning on the table' (I). The light and warmth projected by these two objects symbolises the hope for, and expectancy of, some help from his brother who has not yet arrived, so William takes a seat in a red morocco chair which stands by the fireside. However, when his brother enters the room, he only gives William a very cursory greeting, and takes 'his seat in the morocco-covered armchair, and motioned [him] to another seat'. This act suggests that Edward has no feelings of kindliness and hospitality towards William, and no intention of sharing with him any of his possessions. That this is not an extravagant interpretation of the symbol is confirmed by further references to the fireside in William's observations about his sister-in-law, in which he comments on her physical attractiveness, but then goes on to draw a comparison between exterior glow and inner warmth. He says, 'In sunshine, in prosperity, the flowers are very well; but how many wet days are there in life – November seasons of disaster, when a man's hearth and home would be cold indeed without the clear, cheering gleam of intellect' (I). In this passage the physical warmth radiated by the fire is used as a symbol to express an inner state of spiritual warmth. Further references to the fireside, while William is an employee of his brother, suggest Edward's lack of concern for his employee: 'I repaired to my post in the counting-house as usual; the fire there, but just lit, as yet only smoked; Steighton was not yet arrived' (V). The reason for the tardy lighting of the fire is because Edward does not arrive at the mill until ten o'clock, and when he does 'It was h, custom to glance his eye at Steighton and myself, to hang up his mackintosh, stand a minute with his back to the fire, and then walk out' (V). There is no gesture of warmth or friendliness in any of the encounters between the two brothers; in fact, all William's references to firesides shared with Edward depict Edward as obscuring the warmth, 'with his back to the fire', and William, metaphorically speaking, being left out in the cold. Even the absence of a fire in William's room is a reflection of his intolerable life at the mill, as the following passage shows (IV):

> Thoughts not varied but strong, occupied my mind; two voices spoke within me, again and again they uttered the same monotonous phrases. One said: 'William your life is intolerable'. The other: 'What can you do to alter it?' I walked fast, for it was a cold, frosty night in January; as I approached my lodgings, I turned from a general view of my affairs to the particular speculation as to whether my fire would be out; looking towards the window of my sitting-room, I saw no cheering red gleam.

The absence of a burning fire symbolises his feelings of despair which are embodied in the coldness of his environment, and they are objectified in the absence of a fire. On the other hand, when he is invited in by Mr Hunsden, he notices that in Mr Hunsden's room the 'bright grate was filled with a genuine ——shire fire, red, clear, and generous, no penurious South-of-England embers heaped in the corner of a grate' (IV). Furthermore, there are two easy chairs standing near the fire, so that William and Hunsden can share in the warmth. Thus the fireside has a metaphoric function in signifying the character of its owner, and a symbolic function in defining William's relationship and attitude towards that owner. On another occasion, when William returns to his lodgings, he finds 'a good fire and a clean hearth' (VI), which has been ordered by Mr Hunsden, who is sitting and waiting for him. It is on this occasion that Hunsden gives William an introduction to a Mr Brown, who is living in Brussels, and who will help William to find some work. This reference to the fire symbolises Hunsden's involvement in William's life, but it does not conclude the references to fires in *The Professor*.

Early in the second section of the novel, when William has arrived in Brussels, there is a lengthy passage in which he describes the room in which he takes his breakfast; it is (VII):

> . . . very large and very lofty, and warmed by a stove; the floor was black, and the stove was black, and most of the furniture

was black: yet I never experienced a freer sense of exhilaration than when I sat down at a very long, black table (covered, however, in part by a white cloth), and, having ordered breakfast, began to pour out my coffee from a little black coffee-pot. The stove might be dismal-looking to some eyes, not to mine, but it was indisputably very warm, and there were two gentlemen seated by it talking in French. . . .

These men speak to William in English; I think Charlotte Brontë gives the reader a detailed description of this scene to show in a dramatic manner, and by contrast, William's inhospitable treatment at his brother's house and factory, and the friendliness of strangers in a foreign country. At any rate, despite the strangeness and apparent dreariness of the environment, William is full of confidence and hope, which this passage clearly conveys, dramatically and metaphorically.

In fact, whenever a major change is about to take place in Crimsworth's life, it is introduced in a social context, centred around a fireside. Such an occasion, marking a change in William's life, is when he is invited by Mmes Pelet and Reuter to join then for 'tea', during which ceremony he is offered a post of teacher at a girls' school, of which Mme Reuter's daughter is directress. He accepts the offer, which will have a far-reaching effect on his life, both materially and emotionally. On this occasion he is invited to draw up his chair before the stove, which he does, sitting between the two women, the one representing the boys' school, and the other the girls' school.

On William's first visit to Mlle Henri's room a fire is kindled, which suggests that a relationship is here begun, and to which they contribute equally in order to keep it alive. The passage reflects their mutual feelings (XIX):

I knew she read at once the sort of inward ruth and pitying pain which the chill vacancy of that hearth stirred in my soul: quick to penetrate, quick to determine, and quicker to put into practice, she had in a moment tied a holland apron round her waist; then she disappeared, and reappeared with a basket; it had a cover; she opened it, and produced wood and coal; deftly and compactly she arranged them in the grate. . . She had struck a light; the wood was already in a blaze; and truly, when contrasted with the darkness, the wild tumult of the tempest without, that peaceful glow which began to beam on the now animated hearth, seemed very cheering.

The act of lighting a fire not only reflects Mlle Henri's influence on William's future life, bringing it warmth, love and security from the storms outside, but it also symbolises the beginning of a relationship between them. Another significant fireside scene in William's life is the first fire that Frances lights after their marriage. Again, it is presented as a comparison between the cold outside and the warmth in the room which the fire provides. William describes the scene (XXV):

> It was snowing fast out of doors; the afternoon had turned out wild and cold; the leaden sky seemed full of drifts, and the street was already ankle-deep in the white downfall. Our fire burned bright, our new habitation looked brilliantly clean and fresh, the furniture was all arranged, and there were but some articles of glass, china, books, etc. to put in order.

In this description of domesticity, the fire is an object of joint ownership, which it is the woman's duty to prepare, and for which it is the man's duty to provide the material, and, further, it symbolises the kind of marriage relationship existing between William and Frances: a relationship built on mutual regard and the recognition of mutual obligations. From the foregoing examples it should be clear that Charlotte Brontë uses the 'fireside' as a symbol of social custom, and William's placing to that symbol is indicative of his progress in society both materially and spiritually, at that particular point in his life. To make this quite clear Charlotte Brontë has inserted a passage in which the significance of the fire is explicitly stated. It occurs in the second part of the novel when William unexpectedly returns to Mlle Henri's room, to find that the fire beside which he had been sitting has now been removed (XIX):

> I remarked that Frances had already removed the red embers of her cheerful little fire from the grate: forced to calculate every item, to save in every detail, she had instantly on my departure retrenched a luxury too expensive to be enjoyed alone. 'I am glad it is not yet winter', thought I, 'but in two months more come the winds and rains of November; would to God that before then I could earn the right, and the power, to shovel coals into that grate *ad libitum!*'.

In the Preface Charlotte Brontë states that she had come to prefer what 'was plain and homely', and it is most appropriate that she chose the 'fireside' as a symbol for the home, and by changing the position of her character vis-à-vis the symbol she is able to present social relationships dramatically.

To represent the state of mind and the feelings of a character in terms which can be readily apprehended by the reader, Charlotte Brontë uses natural phenomena as objective correlatives for psychological states, and, sometimes, for the physical state, of the character she is delineating. In *The Professor* this technique is used sparingly, but on each occasion the landscape expresses, in visual imagery, the mental state of the character who is making the observation. The first passage occurs early in the novel. In it there is a clear distinction drawn between the pleasantness of the surrounding countryside of autumn-coloured woods and fields, with a gleaming river cutting through the valley, all of which evokes a sense of harmony in nature, which has now been broken by the intrusion of factory chimneys, that have cut up the landscape and obscured the sky with their smoke. William Crimsworth observes that romance and seclusion have been banished from the landscape, but at this stage it is merely the observation of a fact which does not worry him unduly. However, three months later, when he has had experience of the work his brother has given him to do, and of his brother's conduct towards him, he expresses the unhappiness of his life in a simile drawn from nature, in which the necessity of sunlight for the healthy growth of plants, and for human life, is discussed. He says (IV):

> But this was not all; the antipathy which had sprung up between myself and my employer striking deeper root and spreading denser shade daily, excluded me from every glimpse of the sunshine of life; and I began to feel like a plant growing in humid darkness out of the slimy walls of a well.

Through this simile, drawn from nature, Crimsworth vividly portrays his feeling of despair in the emphasis on darkness; specifically in the total exclusion of sunlight, sunshine being used as a metaphor for joy. The next description of nature occurs after William has been dismissed by Edward, and the passage clearly protrays the change of spirit, the relief, that the loss of employment has effected in William, which he describes as (V):

> A load was lifted off my heart; I felt light and liberated. I had got away from Bigben Close without a breach of resolution; without injury to my self-respect. I had not forced circumstances; circumstances had freed me. Life was again open to me; no longer was its horizon limited by the high black wall surrounding Crimsworth's mill. Two hours had elapsed before my sensations had so far subsided as to leave me calm enough to remark for what wider and clearer boundaries I had exchanged that sooty girdle. When I did look up, Lo! straight before me lay Grovetown, a village of villas about five miles out of X——. The short winter day, as I per-

ceived from the fast-declining sun, was already approaching its
close; a chill frost-mist was rising from the river on which X—
stands, and along whose banks the road I had taken lay; it
dimmed the earth, but did not obscure the clear icy blue of the
January sky. There was a great stillness near and far; the time of
the day favoured tranquillity, as the people were all employed
within-doors, the hour of evening release from the factories not
being yet arrived; a sound of full-flowing water alone pervaded
the air, for the river was deep and abundant, swelled by the
melting of a late snow.

William's sense of release is again presented through nature
imagery; he is now able to look at the sky again. Early in the second
section of the novel, when William is proceeding on his journey to
Brussels, he uses landscape pictures to describe his thoughts and
feelings. He says (VII):

Three – nay, four – pictures line the four-walled cell where are
stored for me the records of the past. First, Eton. All in that
picture is in far perspective, receding, diminutive; but freshly
coloured, green, dewy, with a spring sky, piled with glittering yet
showery clouds; for my childhood was not all sunshine – it had
its overcast, its cold, its stormy hours. Second, X—, huge, dingy;
the canvas cracked and smoked; a yellow sky, sooty clouds; no
sun, no azure; the verdure of the suburbs blighted and sullied – a
very dreary scene. Third, Belgium, and I will pause before this
landscape. As to the fourth, a curtain covers it, which I may here-
after withdraw, or may not, as suits my convenience and capacity.
. . . This is Belgium, reader. Look! don't call the picture a flat
or a dull one – it was neither flat nor dull to me when I first
beheld it . . . I felt like a morning traveller who doubts not that
from the hill he is ascending he shall behold a glowing sunrise. . . .

The variety of scenery which William's eye distinguishes as predominating in the new environment is indicative of his thoughts and
feelings about it. A similar use of nature imagery occurs in the
following passage when William, having obtained a post at M.
Pelet's school, feels free to look at his surroundings (VII):

I might now take some hours of holiday. I felt free to look up.
For the first time I remarked the sparkling clearness of the air,
the deep blue of the sky, the gay, clean aspect of the whitewashed
or painted houses; I saw what a fine street was the Rue Royale. . . .

It is obvious that William is happy, as the emphasis, in this description, is on light and freshness, noted in the air and seen in the buildings. Throughout the novel Charlotte Brontë has used nature to symbolise man's natural state of joy and sorrow, of which the following description of 'The Protestant Cemetery', at Brussels, is another example (XIX):

> My own tread, though slow and upon smooth-rolled paths, seemed to startle, because it formed the sole break to a silence otherwise total. Not only the winds, but the very fitful, wandering airs, were that afternoon, as by common consent, all fallen asleep in their various quarters; the north was hushed, the south silent, the east sobbed not, nor did the west whisper. The clouds in heaven were condensed and dull, but apparently quite motionless. Under the trees of this cemetery nestled warm breathless gloom, out of which the cypresses stood up straight and mute, above which the willows hung low and still; where the flowers, as languid as fair, waited listless for night dew or thunder-shower; where the tombs, and those they hid, lay impassable to sun or shadow, to rain or drought.

The absence of life to be expected in that environment is corroborated in the total suspension of movement in the air, and is further depicted in the drooping vegetation.

That life is a mixture of joy and sorrow is a conviction that Charlotte Brontë frequently expresses in her letters, and it is also a belief symbolised in the novel through her use of metaphors of sun and cloud. One of the early descriptions of Mlle. Henri makes use of sky imagery to convey the mixture of feelings which William sees reflected in her face. He comments (XVI):

> 'Strength and rarity!' I repeated to myself; 'ay, the words are probably true,' for on looking up, I saw the sun has dissevered its screening cloud, her countenance was transfigured, a smile shone in her eyes – a smile almost triumphant; it seemed to say – 'I am glad you have been forced to discover so much of my nature; you need not so carefully moderate your language. Do you think I am myself a stranger to myself? What you tell me in terms so qualified, I have known fully from a child.'

The same observation of Mlle Henri, using the same metaphor, but more explicitly showing William's awakening interest in her, is shown in the following quotation (XVIII):

> Frances did not become pale or feeble in consequence of her

sedentary employment; perhaps the stimulus it communicated to her mind counterbalanced the inaction it imposed on her body. She changed, indeed, changed obviously and rapidly; but it was for the better. When I first saw her, her countenance was sunless, her complexion colourless; she looked like one who had no source of enjoyment, no store of bliss anywhere in the world; now the cloud had passed from her mien, leaving space for the dawn of hope and interest, and those feelings rose like a clear morning, animating what had been depressed, tinting what had been pale. Her eyes, whose colour I had not at first known, so dim were they with repressed tears, so shadowed with ceaseless dejection, now, lit by a ray of the sunshine that cheered her heart, revealed irids of bright hazel – irids large and full, screened with long lashes; and the pupils instinct with fire . . . To speak truth, I watched the change much as a gardener watches the growth of a precious plant, and I contributed to it too, even as the said gardener contributes to the development of his favourite.

Joy and hope are expressed in the sunlight metaphor, but in this passage Charlotte Brontë uses another metaphor as well, to extend the meaning, and bring Crimsworth into the 'picture'. She suggests, in the 'garden' metaphor, that without the assistance of a 'gardener' to aid nature, the plant cannot grow, even if it is surrounded by sunlight. However, the gardener must be sure that the garden upon which he expends his energy is filled with wholesome plants. It is most appropriate that Charlotte Brontë sets William's apprentice-ship to 'gardening' under the guidance of a foreigner, as the grand tour undertaken by young Englishmen after leaving school tradi-tionally included an amatory adventure amidst the art galleries and ruins of foreign countries. Similarly, it is Mlle Reuter who awakens William's masculine instincts. The point of the lesson is that William must learn to distinguish between an artificial 'garden', that of Mlle Reuter, and a natural 'garden', which he finds with Mlle Henri. Most of the second section of the novel is concerned with a portrayal of William's growth in understanding in this regard.

It is significant that during William's first meeting with Mlle Reuter he is allowed to 'view' her garden, whilst on a subsequent visit he is invited to walk in it with her, even returning with a trophy – a branch of lilac. The final mention of Mlle Reuter's garden is when he is in his room looking out upon it, and sees Mlle Reuter and M. Pelet taking a stroll in it. It is on this occasion that he learns that they are engaged, and his comments which appear at the end of the chapter are illuminating of the effect this know-ledge has had. He says, 'Glancing once more towards the long front

of the garden-house, I perceived that its solitary light was at length
extinguished; so, for a time, was my faith in love and friendship'
(XII). But much has taken place in William's life before he reaches
this stage of wisdom.

That Charlotte Brontë purposefully chose a garden as the setting
for William's sexual awakening is suggested by the following remarks when he finds that one of the windows in his austere room
in the Pensionnat Pelet is boarded up. He comments (VII):

> . . . but when M. Pelet had retired and closed the door after him,
> the first thing I did was to scrutinise closely the nailed boards,
> hoping to find some chink or crevice which I might enlarge, and
> so get a peep at the consecrated ground. My researches were vain,
> for the boards were well joined and strongly nailed. It is astonish-
> ing how disappointed I felt. I thought it would have been so
> pleasant to have looked out upon a garden planted with flowers
> and trees, so amusing to have watch the demoiselles at their play;
> to have studied female character in a variety of phases, myself the
> while sheltered from view by a modest muslin curtain. . . .

It is Charlotte Brontë's intention in the novel to show that William
is not allowed to be an observer of the opposite sex, he has to get
into the garden and learn about at least one of them through a
personal contact. On his first visit to Mlle Reuter he describes the
garden that he sees from her salon window; it is (IX):

> . . . a long, not very broad strip of cultured ground, with an alley
> bordered by enormous old fruit-trees down the middle; there was
> a sort of lawn, a parterre of rose-trees, some flower-borders, and,
> on the far side, a thickly-planted copse of lilacs, laburnums, and
> acacias. It looked pleasant, to me – very pleasant, so long a time
> had elapsed since I had seen a garden of any sort. But it was not
> only on Mlle Reuter's garden that my eyes dwelt; when I had
> taken a view of her well-trimmed beds and budding shrubberies,
> I allowed my glance to come back to herself, nor did I hastily
> withdraw it.

It is clear, from the structure of the final sentence, that Charlotte
Brontë is suggesting that there is a connection between the garden
and its owner in William's mind, and that the connection is established through his susceptibilities. Nor is it fortuitous that the chapter following William Crimsworth's view of Mlle Reuter's garden
is a description of his first teaching experience at a girls' school (see
my discussion of this point on pages 15-16). These two chapters
indicate a change in the theme from the earlier part of the novel

where William's economic stability has been the main topic. The remainder of the novel is concerned with sketching his emotional growth, and ends when he has reached his goal – that of marriage to Mlle Henri. William's interest in Mlle Reuter was awakened when he saw the garden through her salon window, but it is only when he is walking with her in the garden, and asks her for 'something', which he then specifies as a 'flower', that we realise the connotations of meaning clustered around the garden image, in this instance epitomised, in the branch of lilac, which she '. . . offered to me with grace. I took it, and went away, satisfied for the present, and hopeful for the future' (XII). That same spring evening William learns that the feelings of the owner of the garden are as artificial as the garden itself. Her token of affection was merely an act of coquetry, and, in fact, she is engaged to M. Pelet. William now knows the mysteries of the garden, the nature of 'the angels and their Eden' (VIII).

There are only two more descriptions of a garden in the novel, and both occur in the final section of the book. The first description is the garden of the Crimsworths in England, and we are told that (XXV):

The garden is chiefly laid out in lawn, formed of the sod of the hills, with herbage short and soft as moss, full of its own peculiar flowers, tiny and starlike, imbedded in the minute embroidery of their fine foliage. At the bottom of the sloping garden there is a wicket, which opens upon a lane as green as the lawn, very long, shady, and little frequented; on the turf of this lane generally appear the first daisies of spring – whence its name – Daisy Lane; serving also as a distinction to the house.

The visual perspective of the garden, in its continuity with the surrounding countryside, is suggested by the presence of natural flowers imbedded in 'the sod of the hills', which has been used to make the garden. It is not like Mlle Reuter's garden, with its high walls, thick shrubbery, and hidden walks; this garden is open and naturally blends into the surrounding countryside.

The last reference to a garden in *The Professor* is on the occasion that the Crimsworths, their son Victor, and Hunsden, take their tea in the garden. In this instance the garden serves as a symbol to indicate the Englishness of the social occasion, and acts as a contrast to the other major experience of Crimsworth's life – his experience in Mlle Reuter's garden. It is aesthetically an apposite use, in which the details of Crimsworth's past life are recalled, but are transcended in the context of the English garden, which differs radically in form and function from the Belgian one.

Literature as an analogy for character or experience is infrequently used in *The Professor*, though the theme of 'the Hill of Difficulty' that William Crimsworth has to climb is taken from Bunyan's *Pilgrim's Progress*. There is one more reference to Bunyan in the novel, in the passage where William describes his reaction to his brother's 'blasphemous sarcasms' by putting on a 'buckler of impenetrable indifference' (III). When William reaches Belgium he describes himself in Keatsian terms as feeling like 'a morning traveller who doubts not that from the hill he is ascending he shall behold a glorious sunrise' (VII). It is appropriate that at this point of her hero's life Charlotte Brontë should use a quotation from a Romantic poet to express William's rise in fortune, and expectation of some 'grand' experience. However, his thoughts are not always romantic, and a Swiftian simile is used to describe the Belgian country-side as 'magnified kitchen-gardens' (XIX). This is in keeping with William's rather critical attitude to the country of which he is a temporary inhabitant. Neither is it inappropriate that Mlle Henri, who is by nature rather puritanical, should make use of a Miltonic simile in a discussion with Hunsden about the importance of one's association with a place. She tells him that (XXIV):

> 'If your world is a world without associations, Mr Hunsden, I no longer wonder that you hate England so. I don't clearly know what Paradise is, and what angels are; yet taking it to be the most glorious region I can conceive, and angels the most elevated existences – if one of them – if Abdiel the Faithful himself' (she was thinking of Milton) 'were suddenly stripped of the faculty of association, I think he would soon rush forth from "the ever-during gates", leave heaven, and seek what he had lost in hell. Yes, in the very hell from which he turned "with retorted scorn".'

It is obvious that, in this passage, the author's views coincide with her character's in expressing the moral necessity for human beings to form emotional attachments to people and places, and certainly she shows that the close association between William and Mlle Henri is superior to the freedom from all emotional and spiritual ties that govern Hunsden's existence. In fact, the comparison of Hunsden's farewell to Mlle Henri as being 'absolutely like Sir Charles Grandison on that of Harriet Byron' (XXIV), is a fine illustration of both personalities, in indicating the courteous and aristocratic qualities in Hunsden, and the puritanical exterior hiding a strong spirit, which is what we see developing in Mlle Henri after her marriage.

It now remains to consider the significance of the selection of these particular visual objects as 'objective correlatives' for thoughts, feelings and experience. Charlotte Brontë wished to present a realistic portrait of a man's efforts to find security from want, and a home in which he would be emotionally fulfilled. Therefore, she chose the fireside, which symbolises the practical, rational aspirations of man, and is itself the product of man's endeavours. The object itself is not poetic, nor is its use beyond the rational. On the contrary, it acts as a signpost indicating William's progress on his self-determined journey. It is an example of the sensitive and subtle use of realism, in which the object used is not encumbered with new meaning, but each one of the traditional meanings is relevant to the context in which it is used. Nature imagery in *The Professor* functions differently to that of the fireside. Firstly, it is used as a sign that there is a prime mover in the universe who controls all activity, both human and non-human, and whose presence can be discerned even in the changing patterns of blue sky and cloud. Secondly, nature is used as a metaphor expressing states of mind and feeling, and both of these functions are aspects of the romantic mode of writing, according to the definition given by Professor Wimsatt:

> . . . romantic nature poetry tends to achieve iconicity by a more direct sensory imitation of something headlong and impassioned, less ordered, nearer perhaps to the subrational . . . we may see metaphysical and neoclassical poetry as near the extreme of logic (though by no means reduced to that status) and romantic poetry as a step towards the directness of sensory presentation (though by no means sunk into subrationality). As a structure which favours implication rather than overt statement, the romantic is far closer than the metaphysical to symbolist poetry and the varieties of postsymbolism most in vogue today.[1]

It is the sensory meanings conveyed by nature images that Charlotte Brontë expects her readers to comprehend in the study of the landscape that she depicts in *The Professor*. The use of literature for comparative purposes in *The Professor* is Charlotte Brontë's most overt mode of communicating information to the reader, as she assumed that the reader would be familiar with the text from which the allusion is drawn, and would, therefore, be able to understand the implications of meaning to the context in which the quotation is used.

Finally, Charlotte Brontë has used the garden allegorically to present William Crimsworth's pre-lapsarian state, when he sees Mlle Reuter's garden. She sets the temptation in the foreign garden, when Mlle Reuter offers him the flower, and sets his post-lapsarian life with Mlle Henri, now Mrs Crimsworth, in an English garden.

Whether Charlotte Brontë had Milton's *Paradise Lost* in mind, or was influenced by her Biblical reading, is unimportant; what is important is to recognise that by using this archetypal metaphor she is able to convey Crimsworth's fall from a state of innocence to the state of ordinary man most effectively, without lengthy passages of narration. Which of the modes, Romanticism or Realism, Charlotte Brontë would choose as the dominant form for her other novels can only be determined after they have been analysed. All that can be affirmed with regard to *The Professor* is that the mode of expression is one of heightened realism, which, in a few passages, reflects an inclination to Romanticism.

3 Jane Eyre

In the novel *Jane Eyre*, the central consciousness is the narrator and heroine Jane Eyre herself, who tells the story of the first thirty years of her life. The autobiographical form that Charlotte Brontë has used, suggesting that it will present a subjective point of view, sets the novel in the Romantic tradition of writing, as it is the essence of Romantic philosophies that man only regards, and singles out for special comment, those aspects of life which are of importance to himself, making use of nature as a visible manifestation of the inward state. Coleridge, who is the most lucid commentator on that mode, states that the Romantic writer strives 'to make the external internal, to make nature thought and thought nature'. This is what Charlotte Brontë has done in *Jane Eyre:* she not only gives the reader a picture of the evolution of Jane from childhood to adulthood, in the external events of education, independence, falling in love, and marriage, but she also depicts the internal changes that take place in Jane's personality at these significant periods of her life. To present the prosaic events of a governess's life, simultaneously with an account of her inward state, at any given point of time, requires a high standard of competency in writing, and in the systematic use of the chosen imagery, if the novel is to show a balance between event and attitude. It is my contention that the novel shows evidence of a greater degree of logical structuring, and a more consistent, consciously made relevant, use of imagery than most critics have recognised or acknowledged. To achieve this unified form, of what could be disparate and extraneous material, Charlotte Brontë has set the narrative of Jane's life within a rigid framework of space and time. Within that structure she has made use of various perspectives and contrasts, which act as reflectors of Jane's personality. Furthermore, there are, as Sylvère Monod painstakingly shows, but incorrectly interprets, thirty occasions on which Jane addresses the reader directly.[1] These moments of interruption in the narrative, when Jane distances herself from the event to turn to a consideration of the possible attitude of the reader, serve as signposts signifying events of singular importance to her, and they also enable Jane to regard her actions objectively. This double perspective, that of the reader on Jane and the latter on her experiences, is also used in the passages in which Jane refers to the books she reads, or when describing the pictures she paints, or the scenery she sees around her, which have both an objective and a subjective frame of reference. They are symptomatic of her state of mind and feeling at that moment, which is their subjective reference, and, simultaneously, they exist, and convey an objective picture.

Finally, there are the passages describing her dreams, which are premonitions of a moral conscience she tries to repress, rather than expressions of wish-fulfilment. These are, in their inherent nature, totally subjective, but not implausible to a character such as Jane's. The only occasion when Charlotte Brontë presumes on the credulity of the reader is the incident when Jane hears Rochester's voice calling her name, and even this is logically linked with a subsequent passage, in which Rochester describes his actions on that particular evening, at the same hour. I do not think that Charlotte Brontë has arbitrarily used this device as a means of ending the novel, as there are references to Jane's powers of extrasensory perception earlier in the novel. There is a paragraph at the beginning of Chapter XXI, in which Jane addresses the reader, rationally discussing the phenomenon of signs and presentiments, and giving her opinion that:

Presentiments are strange things! and so are sympathies; and so are signs: and the three combined make one mystery to which humanity has not yet found the key. I never laughed at presentiments in my life; because I have had strange ones of my own. Sympathies, I believe, exist: (for instance, between far-distant, long-absent, wholly estranged relatives; asserting, notwithstanding their alienation, the unity of the source to which each traces his origin) whose workings baffle mortal comprehension. And signs, for aught we know, may be but the sympathies of Nature with man.

This explanation of a point of view, which is supported by the actions of the speaker, must be accepted by the reader, whatever his or her personal opinion on the subject might be. The critics who object to the 'gothicisms' in *Jane Eyre*, referring, in particular, to the dreams, the voices, and the split chestnut-tree, have not taken into account Jane's natural predisposition to believe in the suprarational, of which we have evidence throughout the novel, beginning in the second chapter, when she thinks she sees a ghostly light in the bedroom of her uncle Reed. It is Charlotte Brontë's intention to depict Jane Eyre as highly imaginative, and super-sensitive, and the author demonstrates these qualities in numerous passages, thus showing that her delineation of Jane's character is consistent. Taking the substance of a letter that Charlotte Brontë wrote to Williams as being a clear statement of her artistic principles, in which is stated that 'The first duty of an author is, I conceive, a faithful allegiance to Truth and Nature; his second, such a conscientious study of Art as shall enable him to interpret eloquently and effectively the oracles delivered by these two great dieties',[2] I think that a more accurate interpretation of the novel can be obtained by studying the artifice employed in presenting Truth and Nature, and certainly it can be affirmed that the structure is not haphazardly formed, nor are the metaphors arbitrarily or injudiciously used.

The most obvious external pattern in *Jane Eyre* is that of place and time. The novel is divided into five geographical sections, which correspond to five major periods of time in the heroine's life. The first section, in which the reader is given a vividly descriptive portrayal of the natural predispositions of the child, begins with Jane, at the age of ten, an orphan, living with her aunt, Mrs Reed, at Gateshead Hall, and ends when she is sent to school. The second section is set in Lowood School. It is here that Jane learns to control her impetuous and passionate nature, through her contact with a fellow pupil, Helen Burns, and also through the influence of the head of the school, Miss Temple. Jane spends eight years at the school, of which the last two years are spent as a teacher. Jane's desire to see more of the outside world leads her to place an advertisement in a local newspaper, in which she offers her services as a governess to a family. She receives one reply – from a Mrs Fairfax, of Thornfield. She is eighteen years old when she proceeds to Thornfield to take up the post. The third section, which covers a period of one year, describes Jane's life as a governess at Thornfield. Although the period covered in this section is short, the range of experience that Jane undergoes here is vast, and is reflected in the size of this section, which comprises approximately 43 per cent of the total novel. It is at Thornfield that the crisis in Jane's life takes place, when she falls in love with her employer, Mr Rochester, who is already married when he offers marriage to Jane. The decision that Jane has to make is between an adulterous life of love, or a life based on fundamental Christian principles. The decision to put her trust in God, and not to follow the dictates of passion, shows the moral progress that Jane has made since her Gateshead days, particularly as she does love Rochester, and she has neither family, friends, nor a place to stay.

The fourth section of the novel is set at Moor House, where Jane arrives after wandering around the countryside without any money for two days. Her stay at Moor House, and in a nearby cottage, covers one year, and begins when she is nearly nineteen years of age. This section depicts Jane having to contend with experiences again differing in nature from those that she has hitherto undergone, the most important being another offer of marriage; this time from a clergyman, St John Rivers, who is eligible, but emotionally cold. Her decision to refuse St John's proposal is based on a very clear-sighted evaluation of her own innate personality, and the passage in which the thought process is described is illuminating of the development that has taken place in Jane since her Gateshead Hall days. She admits that if she were to accept St John, it would mean that [I] (XXXIV):

> must disown half my nature, stifle half my faculties, wrest my tastes from their original bent, force myself to the adoption of pursuits for which I had no natural vocation. He wanted to train me to an elevation I could never reach; [St John wanted Jane to help him with his missionary work in India] it racked me hourly to aspire to the standard he uplifted. The thing was as impossible as to mould my irregular features to his correct and classic pattern, to give to my changeable green eyes the sea-blue tint and solemn lustre of his own.

Her passionate nature, which she acknowledges as being the foundation of her personality, cannot be ignored, although she is tempted to subdue this propensity, and dedicate her life to the service of God. It is at this critical moment that she hears Rochester's voice calling her name, and she decides to return to Thornfield to look for him. The final section of the novel is the shortest. It is set in Ferndean, the country house that Rochester has moved to after Thornfield was destroyed by fire: the fire which also destroys his sight and his left hand, and in which Bertha, his wife, kills herself. Jane is reunited with her Rochester, and they marry. The final chapter projects the story to the present time, when Jane and Rochester have been married for ten years, and ends with a comment on St John, which many critics have found to be incongruous, because they have assumed that Charlotte Brontë intended *Jane Eyre* to be a celebration and vindication of passion, and have not judged the novel on the premises set forth by the author of maintaining 'a faithful allegiance to Truth and Nature'; nature comprising the spiritual, intellectual, and emotional aspects, which together make up the total person – Jane Eyre.

Within this solid structure of space and time which encloses the novel, Charlotte Brontë has depicted Jane's world, of action, thought and feeling; a world which becomes more complex as time progresses and her experiences become more varied, and which constantly requires, on her part, modification of attitudes to the new situations as they arise. At the same time, changes and modifications that take place in Jane's personality, which are seen in her actions, must be shown to be a logical development out of past experience, if the author intends consistently to maintain the conventions required of the autobiographical form of novel. It is my contention that Charlotte Brontë achieves this coherence by using two frames, one which depicts the objective picture, of other people, interiors of houses, natural scenery, Jane's drawings, choice of books, and the mirror reflections of herself, which will be designated as the 'exterior' frame, and the other, which presents a subjective picture of Jane's thoughts, feelings, and attitudes to people, through dreams, and her voices, which will be referred to as the 'interior' frame. These two frames are not kept apart in the novel; frequently the exterior frame is superimposed on the subjective, 'interior' frame, thus establishing a 'composition' of the objective and subjective worlds simultaneously. The writer's purpose in using these two frames is to show what events are of significance to Jane, and her reaction to these events, without going into lengthy passages of introspection and justification; using instead 'objective correlatives' which objectify Jane's thoughts and feelings. The use of such a diversity of 'objective correlatives' would suggest an irrationality on the part of the character, and uncertainty of narrative style and lack of creative vision on the part of the author, if it were not for the fact that there was a definite system determining their use. It is a mode of expression which has some similarity to J. M. W. Turner's technique of painting, about which it has been stated that:

> In spite of the bewildering variety, there is an underlying uniformity of procedure which is what we should expect of a highly professional artist for whom style was always subservient to the compelling demands of creative imagination.[3]

That Charlotte Brontë was familiar with Turner's works we know from Mrs Gaskell, and we also know that from an early age she was interested in art. Therefore, it would not be improbable that, in studying the characteristic style of Turner, she would recognise that a similarly complex technique could be used for the creation of her novels. That Charlotte Brontë has made use of such a method of 'objective correlatives' can be proved by a study of the occasions on which Jane seeks refuge in books; firstly, illustrations, and later story-books. The novel opens with a description of the effect of a winter afternoon's walk on the fingers and toes of a child, and then continues with a description of a cosy drawing-room scene, which the same child looks in upon but is excluded from. These two passages establish the objective world that Jane sees, and the subjective world of her feelings. But Jane is excluded from, in fact is rejected by, that objective world, and so she seeks refuge in the breakfast-room where she can live in her own world, which is 'objectified' in Bewick's 'History of British Birds'. It is significant that the pictures which she singles out for her attention are those which are analogous to her own state; pictures which show the bleak regions of the Arctic, shipwrecks, a graveyard, and a fiend, all of which are emblems of what she feels, but is too young to be able to express in words. That Charlotte Brontë has purposefully used illustrations from books, or the contents of books, as 'objective correlatives' of the feelings of a child who has not the range of experience to express those feelings in verbal form is corroborated by a study of the other occasions when Jane is depicted as reading. The next occasion is the morning after Jane's fainting-fit, which was caused by being locked up in the red room, the room in which her Uncle Reed had died. She is still suffering from the shock of this experience, and is unable to enjoy the special treat that Bessie, the maid, has brought her, so Bessie asks her if she would like to have a book to look at, as she knows that (III)

> . . . the word *book* acted as a transient stimulus, and I begged her to fetch 'Gulliver's Travels' from the library. This book I had again and again perused with delight. I considered it a narrative of facts, and discovered in it a vein of interest deeper than what I found in fairy tales: for as to the elves, having sought them in vain among foxglove leaves and bells, under mushrooms and beneath the ground-ivy mantling old wall-nooks, I had at length made up my mind to the sad truth, that they were all gone out of England to some savage country where the woods were wilder and thicker, and the population more scant; whereas Lilliput and Brobdingnag being, in my creed, solid parts of the earth's surface, I doubted not that I might one day, by taking a long voyage, see with my own eyes the little fields, houses, and trees, the diminutive people, the tiny cows, sheep, and birds of the one realm; and the corn-fields, forest-high, the mighty mastiffs, the monster cats, the tower-like men and women, of the other. Yet when this cherished volume was now placed in my hand – when I turned over its leaves, and sought in its marvellous pictures the charm I had, till now, never failed to find – all was eerie and dreary; the giants were gaunt goblins, and pigmies malevolent and fearful imps, Gulliver a most desolate wanderer in most dread and dangerous regions. I closed the book, which I dared no longer peruse, and put it on the table, beside the untasted tart.

This passage clearly illustrates the use of the double frame, the 'exterior' describing Jane's activity, her study of *Gulliver's Travels*, and in the 'interior' frame we are presented with an account of her state of mind, both frames of reference being objectified in the book she is looking at. By giving the reader an object, here *Gulliver's Travels*, for which there is a previously established response, but to which Jane now reacts differently, the narrator is able to reveal implicitly new states of feeling. The fact that she sees Gulliver 'as a most desolate wanderer' is significant, as at this point her feelings about her own situation are governing her attitude towards what she is reading, and the similarity between herself and Gulliver is too great to make the experience of reading pleasurable. Furthermore, the passage contains clues to Jane's natural predisposition, in her curiosity about the world she has not yet seen, but which she believes to exist in Lilliput and Brobdingnag, and in her preference for this 'real' world to the world of elves and fairies that Bessie has sketched for her in the bedtime stories that she tells her, and, above all, the passage suggests, by the emphasis on the strange and exotic, that Jane has an extremely vivid imagination.

There is only one more reference to Jane Eyre's reading, which occurs after a description of a verbal battle between Jane and Mrs Reed, which Jane wins – it was her first victory in life. However, the feeling of exultation aroused by the victory is followed by pangs of remorse, feelings which she describes by means of a simile drawn from nature (IV): 'a lighted heath, alive, glancing, devouring' expresses her feelings of anger towards Mrs Reed, and a heath 'black and blasted after the flames are dead' expresses her feelings of remorse. To quieten these feelings Jane takes a book (IV):

> . . . some Arabian Tales; I sat down and endeavoured to read. I could make no sense of the subject; my own thoughts swam always between me and the page I had usually found fascinating. I opened the glass-door in the breakfast-room: the shrubbery was quite still: the black frost reigned, unbroken by sun or breeze, through the grounds. I covered by head and arms with the skirt of my frock, and went out to walk in a part of the plantation which was quite sequestered: but I found no pleasure in the silent trees, the falling fir-cones, the congealed relics of autumn, russet leaves, swept by past winds in heaps, and now stiffened together.

In this passage we are told that the book does not hold her attention; this is because its contents are not analogous to her state of mind. Therefore, she goes into the garden, which presents in a visual, concrete form, the desolation, and the 'frost', in her heart. The dreary, grey, empty scene which Jane gazes on metaphorically portrays her own feelings, but it also functions as a moral exemplum, expressing in visual terms what a child's mind can comprehend, that without warmth plants cannot grow and trees will remain bare. The effect of this lesson on Jane is that she puts her arms around Bessie, the first gesture of genuine affection that Jane has ever made. The influence of natural objects on Jane's imagination proves to be a beneficial one as 'That afternoon lapsed in peace and harmony; and in the evening Bessie told me some of her most enchanting stories, and sang me some of her sweetest songs. Even for me life had its gleams of sunshine' (IV). This is the last reference to books in the novel. From now on Charlotte Brontë will make use of Jane's ability to draw and paint as a means of expressing her heroine's state of mind. The change in the kind of 'objective correlative' used is defensible on logical grounds. Jane has grown older, and has now developed some talents of her own, in this instance her art, which will enable her to express her thoughts and feelings more immediately than if she were to point to someone else's picture and say 'this is how I feel'. Furthermore, the passage just quoted marks the beginning of passages of description of nature, which will have a triple function later in the novel. Firstly, they will reflect states of mind, as the quoted passage shows; secondly, they will reflect Jane's sense of the organic unity between man and nature, which begins when she falls in love; and thirdly, they will indicate Jane's spiritual growth, when she recognises in nature the visual embodiment of the infinitude, omnipotence and omnipresence of God. This only takes place after Jane has left Thornfield, and when she needs spiritual reassurance.

But before Jane's eyes are discerning enough to see 'into' nature, a further process of education has to take place, and Charlotte Brontë sets this educative process in the Lowood School section. It is at Lowood that Jane is taught to curb her naturally passionate, and at times, violent nature, through her contact with Helen Burns and Miss Temple. The following passage, which comes after Jane has been publicly exonerated from mendacity by Miss Temple, shows how far she has progressed in her social attitudes, her scholastic abilities, and in exerting self-control. It is also Charlotte Brontë's first reference to Jane's art; she is now sufficiently mature to create her own illustrations of what she thinks and feels. Jane comments (VIII):

Thus relieved of a grievous load, I from that hour set to work afresh, resolved to pioneer my way through every difficulty: I toiled hard, and my success was proportionate to my efforts; my memory, not naturally tenacious, improved with practice: exercise sharpened my wits; in a few weeks I was promoted to a higher class; in less than two months I was allowed to commence French and drawing. I learned the first two tenses of the verb *Etre,* and sketched my first cottage (whose walls, by-the-by, outrivalled in slope those of the leaning tower of Pisa), on the same day. That night, on going to bed, I forgot to prepare in imagination the Barmecide supper of hot roast potatoes, or white bread and new milk, with which I was wont to amuse my inward cravings: I feasted instead on the spectacle of ideal drawings, which I saw in the dark; all the work of my own hands: freely pencilled houses and trees, picturesque rocks and ruins, Cuyp-like groups of cattle, sweet paintings of butterflies hovering over unblown roses, of birds picking at ripe cherries, of wrens' nests enclosing pearl-like eggs, wreathed about with young ivy sprays.

Jane's relief in being accepted as a worthy member of the community at Lowood, and her sense of belonging to it, is reflected in the subject matter she chooses for her imaginary drawings; happy scenes of domesticity, and the benign aspects of nature. There is one more reference to Jane's artistic efforts at the close of the Lowood section, when Bessie comes to visit her, and asks her if she can draw. Jane points to a painting hanging over the chimneypiece in the parlour: it is a landscape which Jane has given to the superintendent of the school as an acknowledgement for her assistance in getting a reference from the school committee, and which the superintendent has had glazed and framed. Bessie's comment is indicative of Jane's progress. She says, ' "Well, that is beautiful, Miss Jane! It is as fine a picture as any Miss Reed's drawing-master could paint, let alone the young ladies themselves, who could not come near it: and have you learnt French?" ' (X). To the question Jane can also answer in the affirmative. This short passage of dialogue is illuminating of Jane Eyre's progress on two levels: firstly her educational achievements, shown in her proficiency in art and French, and, secondly, in self-control and tranquillity of spirit, which is reflected in the subject chosen for the painting. In this passage we see Charlotte Brontë most effectively using both the subjective and the objective frames as a means of presenting, through illustration, the personality of the eighteen-year-old girl. Having established this mode of narration, by showing the need in Jane for some form of self-expression, it is not surprising that Charlotte Brontë uses this method again in the Thornfield section. Thus, the passage in which Jane is described as showing her portfolio of water-colours to Rochester, on the first occasion that she spends an evening in his company, is logical in terms of the character, as we have learned to know her in the previous sections of the novel, and is also an effective means of objectively expressing the workings of Jane's mind and heart, especially as she is reticent and shy. It must also be remembered that these pictures were executed during the Lowood period of her life, thus they represent something of her past experience at Lowood, as well as at Gateshead. The pictures that Rochester singles out for particular attention are three studies of nature, each one being a composition in which a human face or body is shown against a background of natural scenery. The first picture is a scene at sea, with one gleam of light shining on the mast of a foundered ship. On the mast a cormorant is sitting, with a gold bracelet in his beak, and shadowed in the water is a drowned corpse. The second picture is of a hill rising into a twilight-coloured sky, with a shadowy picture of a woman's shape merging into the sky. The only illumination in the picture comes from a star on her forehead, and a suggestion of moonlight trying to pierce the driving clouds. The third picture is of an iceberg with, in the foreground, a colossal head resting on it. The lower part of the face is veiled, but on the forehead there is a ring of light interspersed with sparkling gems.' That these pictures communicate something of Jane's past to Rochester is substantiated by his comment, ' "Not quite" '. This is in response to her observation that she had been unable to express what was in her mind. He then continues (XIII):

. . . you have secured the shadow of your thought: but no more, probably. You have not enough of the artist's skill and science to give it full being: yet the drawings are, for a schoolgirl, peculiar. As to the thoughts, they are elfish. These eyes in the Evening Star you must have seen in a dream. How could you make them look so clear, and yet not at all brilliant? for the planet above quells their rays. And what meaning is that in their solemn depth? And who taught you to paint wind? There is a high gale in that sky, and on this hilltop. Where did you see Latmos? For that is Latmos. There, – put the drawings away!

The three pictures that Rochester is looking at have a common theme – they all symbolise feelings of death. The first painting was probably derived from the recollection of a picture seen in Bewick's 'History of British Birds', and though it was painted at Lowood, it might very well symbolise Jane's predominating feelings while at Gateshead. The second picture appears to embody Jane's feelings at Lowood, after the departure of Miss Temple, when a feeling of restriction and exclusion from the world outside, drove her to advertise her services as a governess. The quotation from Milton's *Paradise Lost* gives the reader a clue as to the meaning of the third picture; it is that of the figure of Death, in Book II. Thus the pictures reveal something of Jane's feelings during the Gateshead and Lowood periods of her life. Rochester's interpretation of, and response to, these paintings is also significant, as it gives the reader a clue as to his thoughts and feelings – indicated by the question ' "Where did you see Latmos? For that is Latmos" ' – and suggests that he had the Endymion legend in mind. In the legend the moon is in love with Endymion, and puts him into perpetual sleep. That is the literal basis for Keats's poem *Endymion,* but on an allegorical

level the poem symbolises the poet's melancholy longing, either for
an early death, or for a life of poetry. Both the implied literary
references, to Milton and to Keats, are appropriate to Jane at this
point, when her emotional and spiritual sensibilities have been
awakened, and it explains why the pictures are described in the
Thornfield section and not in the Lowood section. It also explains
Rochester's abrupt request to ' "put the drawings away" ', as the
legend of Latmos is expressive of his life hitherto. It is also obvious
that Rochester is intrigued by the mind and feelings of the artist,
represented by these illustrations, which convey a total picture of
the personality far more effectively than would pages of explanation
or dialogue. In this way Charlotte Brontë has made a symbol out
of Jane's art, expressing thought and feeling. This technique is
built into the novel from the first chapter, but Charlotte Brontë
systematically uses different modes of representation and illustration; first, analogously, in the books she selects, secondly, symbolically, in the paintings she creates, and, finally, analogously, symbolically and metaphorically, in the descriptions of nature imagery which
Jane's eye observes, and with which her heart and mind empathe-
sise.

Before a detailed discussion of the function of landscape as a
narrative technique in *Jane Eyre* is discussed, it is necessary to consider Charlotte Brontë's further references to Jane's art, and the
function they play in the depiction of personality. The next reference to art occurs in the Thornfield section; it is when Jane paints
two portraits, one of herself '. . . a Governess, disconnected, poor,
and plain', and the other of Miss Ingram, based on a description
that Mrs Fairfax has given her, of a tall girl with a '. . . fine bust,
sloping shoulders, long graceful neck; olive complexion, dark and
clear; noble features, eyes rather like Mr Rochester's, large and
black, and as brilliant as her jewels. And then she had such a fine
head of hair, raven-black, and so becomingly arranged; a crown of
thick plaits behind, and in front the longest, the glossiest curls I
ever saw' (XVI). Both the portraits are, to an extent, an exaggerated
configuration of the difference between herself and Blanche, but
that the difference exists cannot be questioned, nor the fact that she
sees Blanche as a rival. What the passage also shows is a change in
Jane; she is now more concerned in using her art to represent the
world of actuality, and not the world of her imagination, and Charlotte Brontë has made use of the artistic ability of her character to
show that Jane is involved with a real situation.

A further reference to Jane's art is when she has temporarily left
Thornfield to visit the Reeds at Gateshead, as her aunt is dying. In
order to occupy the time between the infrequent visits to her aunt
Jane busied herself 'in sketching fancy vignettes, representing any

scene that happened momentarily to shape itself in the ever-shifting kaleidoscope of imagination: a glimpse of sea between two rocks; the rising moon, and a ship crossing its disk; a group of reeds and water-flags, and a naiad's head crowned with lotus-flowers, rising out of them; an elf sitting in a hedge-sparrow's nest, under a wreath of hawthorn-bloom' (XXI). From these precise pictures which symbolise Jane's thoughts and feelings about her change of status in the Reed family – she has risen above them – her mind turns to Mr Rochester, and she 'fell to sketching a face: what sort of a face it was to be, I did not care or know', but when it was completed 'I had a friend's face under my gaze; and what did it signify that those young ladies turned their backs on me? I looked at it; I smiled at the speaking likeness: I was absorbed and content.' This description of Jane's artistic activity, of her fanciful pictures as well as her portrait, serves to synthesise, in a visual form, the progress and change that has taken place in Jane's life, as the sea, rising moon, and ship pictures are allusions to her childhood at Gateshead, memories of which are reawakened by the visit, while the naiad's head and elf are a pictorial representation of Rochester's descriptions of her at Thornfield, who frequently uses these epithets when referring to Jane. It is perfectly logical, therefore, that her drawing should culminate in the picture of Rochester, the man who had radically altered her vision of life. To present that change of outlook by means of symbols suggestive of her past as well as her present life, shows something of the range of Charlotte Brontë's own powers of artistic expression.

There is only one more reference to Jane's drawing. The passage occurs in the Moor House section, and describes Rosamund Oliver finding some of Jane's sketches 'including a pencil-head of a pretty little cherub-like girl, one of my scholars, and sundry views from nature, taken in the Vale of Morton and on the surrounding moors' (XXXII). Rosamund is impressed with the quality of the work, and asks Jane to sketch a portrait of herself. This Jane does, and shows the finished picture to St John Rivers, who is in love with Rosamund, and who concedes that the portrait is a correct likeness of the subject. Jane's emotional involvement with this work is only the pleasure derived from the accurate depiction of a pretty face, and thus the picture has none of the 'Romantic' or 'impressionistic' qualities of her other paintings. She is completely objective here.

When she is reunited with Rochester, and living at Ferndean Manor, her artistic activities find a new medium of expression in the use of images which are true and natural – they are no longer visual embodiments of morbid fantasies. This new artistic mode is both an accurate transcription of what the eye sees, and it also emblematically represents Jane's new state. She relates (XXXVIII):

Mr Rochester continued blind the first two years of our union: perhaps it was that circumstance that drew us so very near – that knit us so very close! for I was then his vision, as I am still his right hand. Literally, I was (what he often called me) the apple of his eye. He saw nature – he saw books through me; and never did I weary of gazing for his behalf, and of putting into words the effect of field, tree, town, river, cloud, sunbeam – of the landscape before us; of the weather round us – and impressing by sound on his ear what light could no longer stamp on his eye.

Jane has found fulfilment and tranquillity as Rochester's wife, and the talent which she formerly used to express her thoughts and feelings is now diverted to an altruistic act, in making Rochester's world meaningful. In the drawing together, and finishing, of this facet of Jane, Charlotte Brontë has shown her mastery over what to many critics appears to be an extraneous element in the novel, and has herself created a work of art, by the manner in which she incorporates this talent and shows it to be an integral part of the personality of Jane Eyre. Jane's eye for landscape, to which the passage just quoted refers, is not an interest she develops only after marriage.

From the beginning of the Thornfield section, in fact, we find that Charlotte Brontë frequently uses natural landscape as a means of objectifying Jane's thoughts and feelings, which formerly were expressed through the books she read and the pictures she painted. This seems to me to be an extremely appropriate and subtle medium through which to show the expansion of vision, both objective and subjective, that takes place in Jane. The technique of portraying visually the expansion of Jane's horizon is an adaptation taken from the romantic artists who endeavoured to relate landscape to human life. Thus, by altering the perspective of Jane's world from the interior of houses, which predominates in the first two sections of the novel, Charlotte Brontë is enabled to suggest the growth of personality in her character. In the first two sections of the novel there are only two descriptions of nature. One is the passage which has already been discussed (see page 37), and the other occurs in the Lowood section. It is a description of the first occasion that Jane looks at nature objectively, and she finds that (IX):

. . . a great pleasure, an enjoyment which the horizon only bounded, lay all outside the high and spike-guarded walls of our garden: this pleasure consisted in prospect of noble summits girdling a great hill-hollow, rich in verdure and shadow; in a bright beck, full of dark stones and sparkling eddies. How different had this scene looked when I viewed it laid out beneath the iron sky of winter, stiffened in frost, shrouded with snow! – when mists as chill as death wandered to the impulse of east winds along those purple peaks, and rolled down 'ing' and holm till they blended with the frozen fog of the beck! That beck itself was then a torrent, turbid and curbless: it tore asunder the wood, and sent a raving sound through the air, often thickened with wild rain or whirling sleet; and for the forest on its banks, *that* showed only ranks of skeletons.

What this passage shows is that Jane is now able to make a comparison between her recollection of the past winter, and the present view of the same terrain in its summer green, and, by implication, she can make the same distinction between her periods of 'frost', which is the symbol used in the Gateshead section, with the present 'green' of Lowood. Furthermore, the passage objectifies, in a very subtle manner, the expansion of Jane's mental and emotional faculties. In fact, not only nature is used to symbolise her widening horizon, but colour also is used by Charlotte Brontë to illuminate her feelings of happiness. Thus nature in its diversity of form and colour is used objectively to provide the reader with a focal point which is independent of the character in the novel, and, at the same time, that same landscape is used as a visual metaphor illustrative of the thoughts and feelings of the character; furthermore, in this passage, the transitoriness to be seen in nature is implied to be analogous to the life of a human being, thus a symbolic significance is given to nature.

From the Thornfield section onwards nature is always used as an 'objective correlative' for Jane's inward state. However, to discuss all the passages in which nature is described would make this section too unwieldy, and it is my intention to take only a representative selection to show how Charlotte Brontë uses nature as the outward manifestation of an inward state, and how Jane's mental, spiritual, and emotional progress can be measured by the expansion of her visual horizon. The first passage occurs early in the Thornfield section; the name 'Thornfield' is itself significant, as it denotes both the harsh and the genial aspects of nature, and this ambivalence in nature is also reflected in the human condition, that of joy and sorrow. The following passage occurs before Jane has met Rochester; she is describing a winter's afternoon walk (XII):

The ground was hard, the air was still, my road was lonely; I walked fast till I got warm, and then I walked slowly to enjoy and analyse the species of pleasure brooding for me in the hour and situation. It was three o'clock; the church bell tolled as I passed under the belfry: the charm of the hour lay in its

approaching dimness, in the low-gliding and pale-beaming sun.
I was a mile from Thornfield, in a lane noted for wild roses in
summer, for nuts and blackberries in autumn, and even now
possessing a few coral treasures in hips and haws, but whose best
winter delight lay in its utter solitude and leafless repose. If a
breath of air stirred, it made no sound here; for there was not a
holly, not an evergreen to rustle, and the stripped hawthorn and
hazel bushes were as still as the white, worn stones which cause-
wayed the middle of the path. Far and wide, on each side, there
were only fields, where no cattle now browsed; and the little
brown birds, which stirred occasionally in the hedge, looked like
single russet leaves that had forgotten to drop.

This landscape presents a picture of suspended life, in the absence
of sound (except for the church bell ringing out the time), very
little movement, and an overall dimness of light, and yet it is a
picture of tranquillity, which corresponds to Jane's own state. It is
also interesting to note the placing of this passage, which follows a
comment of Jane's to the reader on the need for human beings to
have action, they cannot be satisfied with tranquillity (see Chapter
XII). From the sensory details of sight and sound given in this
passage the reader can extrapolate Jane's sensitivity to nature, and
her state of heightened awareness towards her surroundings, but her
eyes are earth-bound. However, shortly after this moment she meets
Rochester, and the description of nature after the meeting shows
how her horizon has widened. She does not want to go inside the
house (XII):

. . . both my eyes and spirit seemed drawn from the gloomy house
– from the grey hollow filled with rayless cells, as it appeared to
me – to the sky expanded before me – a blue sea absolved from
taint of cloud; the moon ascending it in solemn march; her orb
seeming to look up as she left the hilltops, from behind which she
had come, far and farther below her, and aspired to the zenith
midnight-dark in its fathomless depth and measureless distance:
and for those trembling stars that followed her course; they made
my heart tremble, my veins glow when I viewed them. Little
things recall us to earth: the clock struck in the hall; that sufficed: I turned from moon and stars, opened a side door, and
went in.

Jane has undergone a new dimension of experience, which is
reflected in the changed angle of vision, from the vertical plane to
the horizontal. In fact, this passage marks the beginning of the inclusion of sky imagery with the landscape in Jane's vision of her

world. The sky represents the world of the spirit, and within that metaphor the moon is distinguished as the symbol of love.

That the moon images the spiritual quality of Jane's love is shown in the following passage, which occurs after her engagement to Rochester, but before the disastrous marriage ceremony. Jane is in the garden looking at the blasted chestnut-tree, and while she is looking at the two charred sections 'the moon appeared momentarily in that part of the sky which filled their fissure; her disk was blood-red and half overcast; she seemed to throw on me one bewildered, dreary glance, and buried herself again instantly in the deep drift of cloud. The wind fell, for a second, round Thornfield; but far away over wood and water, poured a wild, melancholy wail: it was sad to listen to, and I ran off again' (XXV). The unnatural appearance of the moon is portentous of the proposed marriage which is shortly to take place; and the entire passage is an allegory on that marriage. At this stage Jane ignores the omen from the spiritual world, but when she leaves Thornfield, and is forced to spend the first night in the open, she realises heaven, earth and man are all part of one universe, and she finally acknowledges her belief in the infinitude of God (XXVIII):

> Night was come, and her planets were risen: a safe, still night; too serene for the companionship of fear. We know that God is everywhere, but certainly we feel His presence most when His works are on the grandest scale spread before us: and it is in the unclouded night-sky, where His worlds wheel their silent course, that we read clearest His infinitude, His omnipotence, His omnipresence. I had risen to my knees to pray for Mr Rochester. Looking up, I, with tear-dimmed eyes, saw the mighty Milky Way. Remembering what it was – what countless systems there swept space like a soft trace of light – I felt the might and strength of God. Sure was I of His efficiency to save what He had made: convinced I grew that neither earth should perish nor one of the souls it treasured.

The question that Jane asks of Helen Burns, 'Where is God?', 'What is God?' she herself finds the answer to in nature; nature has been her teacher, as it will be her guardian, and her nurse. This passage marks the end of Charlotte Brontë's use of natural phenomena as 'objective correlatives' for Jane's states of mind and feeling. This is because Jane is now totally in tune with nature, and all that nature represents, and, therefore, nature can no longer be used as a perspective whereby Jane's progress – mental, emotional, and spiritual – can be viewed. The subjective and objective frames have been fused to form a single picture – of Jane's universe.

That Charlotte Brontë had the reader in mind while writing the novel is obvious from the passages addressed directly to the reader which occur throughout the novel, and which have been briefly commented upon on page 31. These apostrophes to the reader enable the narrator to detach herself from the event, and provide Charlotte Brontë with a means of depicting the purely subjective and partial responses of the growing girl without leaving the reader in any doubt as to how much weight to put on her words. For the writer it is a very important and liberating method of presenting a double stance – in which past and present attitudes can be depicted simultaneously – as it must be remembered that the narrative is recounted retrospectively from a distance of ten years. Another technique she has used to present Jane objectively is to make use of other characters as commentators on Jane's appearance and behaviour. A conversation between Bessie and Miss Abbot, in the Gateshead section, tells the reader how she appears through other eyes. Miss Abbot says, ' " if she were a nice, pretty child, one might compassionate her forlornness; but one really cannot care for such a little toad as that" '. This is an opinion which Bessie supports by the following comment, ' "at any rate, a beauty like Miss Georgina would be more moving in the same condition" ' (III). Charlotte Brontë has made her point – that Jane is not a beauty, nor does she have winning ways to evoke sympathy from other people.

Running parallel with the comments of other characters there is also the mirror device, which Charlotte Brontë has used to give the reader another kind of objective view of Jane. By describing how Jane sees herself in the mirror, she has hit on a method of externalising Jane's thoughts about herself, and thus the mirror serves to objectify subjective states of mind in an immediate and concrete image. The first mirror image of Jane is when she is locked in the red room, the room where her uncle Reed died, and the picture that the mirror reflects is of a '. . . strange little figure there gazing at me, with a white face and arms specking the gloom, and glittering eyes of fear moving where all else was still, had the effect of a real spirit: I thought it like one of the tiny phantoms, half fairy, half imp, Bessie's evening stories represented as coming out of lone, ferny dells in moors, and appearing before the eyes of belated travellers' (II). Jane sees herself as a small spirit-being who does not belong to the world represented by Gateshead. The reflected picture makes her even more fearful, and this stimulates her already overwrought imagination to even more bitter thoughts about the Reeds.

Charlotte Brontë, in using the mirror reflection method, is able to make explicit Jane's thoughts about her situation, and to show a little more of Jane's natural disposition. It is at Lowood School that a new facet of Jane's character is described; this is by Helen Burns who remarks that 'I observed you in your class this morning, and saw that you were closely attentive: your thoughts never seemed to wander while Miss Miller explained the lesson and questioned you' (VI). This information helps the reader to understand that Jane's scholastic progress at Lowood is due to her attitude towards learning. It also makes explicit developing qualities of self-control, which Jane will need at Thornfield. On the other hand, her natural propensities are also noticed by Helen Burns, who comments on Jane's uncivilised, and pagan, attitudes: she says, ' " You will change your mind, I hope, when you are older: as yet you are but a little untaught girl" ', and urges Jane to ' "Read the New Testament, and observe what Christ says, and how he acts; make his word your rule, and his conduct your example" ' (VI). This is a moral precept which Jane adopts and acts upon later in life, when she returns to Gateshead to visit the dying Mrs Reed, and tells her ' "Many a time, as a little child, I should have been glad to love you if you would have let me; and I long earnestly to be reconciled to you now: kiss me, aunt" '. Even though Mrs Reed rejects her request, Jane tells her that she has ' "my full and free forgiveness" ' (XXI).

On the next occasion, after the 'picture' episode, that Jane spends an evening with Mr Rochester, the reader is given a description of Jane as she appears to other people, in this case Mr Rochester. He says (XIV):

Do you never laugh, Miss Eyre? Don't trouble yourself to answer – I see, you laugh rarely; but you can laugh very merrily: believe me, you are not naturally austere, any more than I am naturally vicious. The Lowood constraint still clings to you somewhat; controlling your features, muffling your voice, and restricting your limbs; and you fear in the presence of a man and a brother – or father, or master, or what you will – to smile too gaily, speak too freely, or move too quickly: but, in time, I think you will learn to be natural with me, as I find it impossible to be conventional with you; and then your looks and movements will have more vivacity and variety than they dare offer now. I see at intervals the glance of a curious sort of bird through the close-set bars of a cage; a vivid, restless, resolute captive is there; were it but free, it would soar cloud-high.

Not only are Rochester's observations about Jane's present conduct true, as she does seem to glide quietly around Thornfield observing the behaviour of the other inhabitants, whilst being somewhat withdrawn herself, but also his prognosis of her potential joyousness and merriment is accurate, as the Ferndean section will show. Furthermore, Jane's mirror also reflects a change in her appearance since her arrival at Thornfield, as she observes of herself 'Bessie Leaven had said I was quite a lady; and she spoke truth: I was a lady. And now I looked much better than I did when Bessie saw me: I had more colour and more flesh, more life, more vivacity; because I had brighter hopes and keener enjoyments' (XVI). Charlotte Brontë has used the device of commentaries of other characters to present an objective picture of Jane, and mirrors to objectify subjective states of feeling. Most frequently, the comments are about her character or behaviour whilst the mirror reflects her appearance and attitude, but, studied in conjunction with her own actions and explanations, they provide the reader with a rounded picture of the character.

The next time that Rochester comments on Jane he is disguised as a gipsy, which allows him complete freedom; he tells her (XIX):

> I see no enemy to a fortunate issue but in the brow; and that brow professes to say, – 'I can live alone, if self-respect and circumstances require me so to do. I need not sell my soul to buy bliss. I have an inward treasure, born with me, which can keep me alive if all extraneous delights should be withheld; or offered only at a price I cannot afford to give.' The forehead declares 'Reason sits firm and holds the reins, and she will not let the feelings burst away and hurry her to wild chasms. The passions may rage furiously, like true heathens, as they are; and the desires may imagine all sorts of vain things: but judgement shall still have the last word in every argument, and the casting vote in every decision. Strong wind, earthquake-shock, and fire may pass by: but I shall follow the guiding of that still small voice which interprets the dictates of conscience.'

Not only are these comments an accurate observation of innate qualities of character in Jane, but they also prepare the reader for subsequent events, when these qualities of character will be presented in a dramatic form; this is when Jane has to decide whether she will live with Rochester as his mistress, or to reject this limited form of love, and leave him. Rochester's interpretation of phrenology here justifies the decision that she subsequently makes. This passage is a further example of the objectivity with which Charlotte Brontë visualises character, seen in the narrative method she employs, by presenting facets of the character through the observations of other people, and then purposefully portraying these qualities in action.

The morning after the engagement to marry Rochester Jane looks at herself in the mirror, and notices that the reflection of her face shows (XXIV):

> . . . It was no longer plain: there was hope in its aspect, and life in its colour; and my eyes seemed as if they had beheld the fount of fruition, and borrowed beams from the lustrous ripple. I had often been unwilling to look at my master, because I feared he could not be pleased at my look; but I was sure I might lift my face to his now, and not cool his affection by its expression. I took a plain but clean and light summer dress from my drawer and put it on: it seemed no attire had ever so well become me; because none had I ever worn in so blissful a mood.

The transforming power of happiness, in which plainness is not changed into beauty, but is transformed by a radiance coming from the soul, is a completely correct and rational observation. This passage demonstrates the perspicuity with which Charlotte Brontë observes human beings, and also validates her claim that it is morally wrong to make the heroine beautiful as a matter of course, as she believes that beauty is not a necessary quality for an interesting character.

Harriet Martineau, in her obituary on Charlotte Brontë, gives the reader some information on Charlotte's ideas on heroines; she relates (Allott: 303):

> *Jane Eyre* was naturally and universally supposed to be Charlotte herself; but she always denied it, calmly, cheerfully, and with the obvious sincerity which characterized all she said. She declared that there was no more ground for the assertion than this. She once told her sisters they were wrong – even morally wrong – in making their heroines beautiful, as a matter of course. They replied that it was impossible to make a heroine interesting on other terms. Her answer was, 'I will prove to you that you are wrong. I will show you a heroine as small and plain as myself who shall be as interesting as any of yours.' 'Hence, *Jane Eyre*', she said in telling the anecdote; 'but she is not myself, any further than that.'

That Jane Eyre is not Charlotte Brontë, but is the embodiment of a person created by Charlotte's imagination, is clearly stated in this passage, and must be accepted as fact. But to return to the creation: Mrs Fairfax is also used as a commentator on Jane, and her opinions expressed to Jane, after she has been told by Rochester of the engagement, are that (XXIV):

. . . you are very well; and much improved of late: and Mr
Rochester, I daresay, is fond of you. I have always noticed that
you were a sort of pet of his. There are times when, for your
sake, I have been a little uneasy at his marked preference, and
have wished to put you on your guard: but I did not like to
suggest even the possibility of wrong. I knew such an idea would
shock, perhaps offend you; and you were so discreet, and so
thoroughly modest and sensible, I hoped you might be trusted to
protect yourself.

Mrs Fairfax's observations reinforce the reader's interpretations of
Jane, which have been established in the previous passages.

There is only one more mirror reflection described, and this is a
picture of Jane in her wedding clothes. She is about to hurry down
to go with Rochester to the church, but is told by Sophie, the maid,
to look in the mirror before she leaves, and sees '. . . a robed and
veiled figure, so unlike my usual self that it seemed almost the image
of a stranger' (XXVI). The reflection appears strange to Jane, because the person reflected in the mirror is not dressed according to
her conception of her person and status, but is dressed as Rochester
imagines her to be, a kind of sprite, elf or fairy; descriptive terms
which he uses constantly when speaking to, and about, Jane, and
which are as unrealistic, as his later attempts to dress her as a beauty
– delicate and aerial – show. But the image is also one of those
prophetic or ominous images – Jane is a stranger to herself because
she is not to be a bride. It evokes a sense of foreboding and mis-
giving. This passage clearly illustrates my contention that Charlotte
Brontë's narrative techniques are more subtle than critics have given
her credit for, as the fact that she makes Jane describe herself as a
'stranger' to herself shows that the author had the total plot and
characterisation pattern in her mind when she wrote this passage.

There are only two more passages in *Jane Eyre* where other
characters comment on the heroine. The first passage occurs in the
Moor House section (XXIX), when Hannah, the Rivers' servant,
reproaches Jane for not being able to keep herself, a criticism which
she resents, reminding Hannah of the Christian belief that desti-
tution is not a crime. This has been interpreted by one critic[5] as an
instance of the lack of systematic character portrayal in the novel,
as the moral principles of Jane's argument, upon which this passage
is based, differ from an earlier passage, when Jane is talking to Mr
Lloyd, the apothecary. In this passage she says that she does not
want to go to her 'poor' Eyre relations because 'I could not see how
poor people had the means of being kind; and then to learn to
speak like them, to adopt their manners, to be uneducated, to grow
up like one of the poor women I saw sometimes nursing their chil-

dren or washing their clothes at the cottage doors of the village of Gateshead: no, I was not heroic enough to purchase liberty at the price of caste' (III). Certainly, there is a change in her point of view between the Gateshead days and Moor House, but I think this can be read as a dramatisation of the change that has taken place in Jane Eyre, which is, I think, what Charlotte Brontë intended to show; that is, how far Jane has journeyed on the road to spiritual maturity. In any case, the placing of this passage is entirely logical when considered as following her actions at Thornfield, as much as it would have been implausible in the Gateshead section, before the educational process at Lowood had taken place. I believe the function of the Moor House passage is to prepare the reader for Jane's acceptance of a disabled man for a husband; at any rate, it shows a facet of Jane's character which the reader has not hitherto seen.

The final passage in *Jane Eyre* in which another character reports on Jane, is a recapitulation of her life at Thornfield, and relates how the servants saw her relationship with Rochester (XXXVI):

The servants say they never saw anybody so much in love as he was: he was after her continually. They used to watch him — servants will, you know, ma'am — and he set store on her past everything: for all, nobody but him thought her so very handsome. She was a little small thing, they say, almost like a child. I never saw her myself; but I've heard Leah, the housemaid, tell of her. Leah liked her well enough. Mr Rochester was about forty, and this governess not twenty; and you see, when gentlemen of his age fall in love with girls, they are often like as if they were bewitched: well, he would marry her.

Jane also learns from him of the fire at Thornfield, the death of Rochester's wife, and that he is living alone. The passage serves to recall to mind past events, to clarify what has taken place in Rochester's life during Jane's absence, and to prepare the reader for a new, chastened man; it functions both as a summary of the past, and as an introduction to the future.

It only remains to consider the necessity for, and appropriateness of, the 'gothic' passages; the passages in which the reader is told about Jane's vision of a ghostly light, her reveries, dreams, and the voice she hears: to decide whether these instances of the supernatural are explicable on rational grounds, when the full facts are known, or, alternatively, whether they are justified in terms of characterisation when the inherent nature of the person is considered. From the beginning of the autobiography we are told, by Jane, that she is superstitious, and we know from the pictures she chooses to look at, in Bewick's 'History of British Birds', that she has a strong imagination, and we are also told that Bessie has stimulated that imagination with bedtime stories about 'tiny phantoms'; it seems entirely in character, therefore, that the ten-year-old child when seeing a moving light in the red room imagines it to be 'a herald of some coming vision from another world' (II). The narrator, at a distance of twenty years later, suggests that the most likely explanation for the light is that it was the gleam of a lantern, carried by someone going across the lawn, but this kind of rationalisation would be improbable to a small child who is fearful, oppressed, and very sensitive, and, therefore, her reaction to the light seems entirely justified. This episode dramatises that Jane is super-sensitive, and that she has a very active imagination, and it is her imagination, stimulated by her new surroundings when at Thornfield, which leads her to dream about a visionary world, as she relates (XII):

I climbed the three staircases, raised the trap-door of the attic, and having reached the leads, looked out afar over sequestered field and hill, and along dim sky-line – that then I longed for a power of vision which might overpass that limit; which might reach the busy world, towns, regions full of life I had heard of but never seen: that then I desired more of practical experience than I possessed; more of intercourse with my kind, of acquaintance with variety of character, than was here within my reach. I valued what was good in Mrs Fairfax, and what was good in Adèle; but I believed in the existence of other and more vivid kinds of goodness, and what I believed in I wished to behold.
. . . Then my sole relief was to walk along the corridor of the third story, backwards and forwards, safe in the silence and solitude of the spot and allow my mind's eye to dwell on whatever bright visions rose before it – and, certainly, they were many and glowing; to let my heart be heaved by the exultant movement, which, while it swelled it in trouble, expanded it with life; and, best of all, to open my inward ear to a tale that was never ended – a tale my imagination created, and narrated continuously; quickened with all of incident, life, fire, feeling, that I desired and had not in my actual existence.

Jane's indulgence in reveries is a normal activity in the process of growing up, which will disappear when real life provides her with sufficient material for her active imagination to work upon. Her first encounter with something strange and real is the inexplicable presence of Grace Poole on the third floor of Thornfield, and her second experience is her encounter with a large dog, followed by a figure on a horse, who turns out to be her employer, Mr Rochester, but which she had for a moment thought was a 'North-of-England spirit, called a "Gytrash", which, in the form of horse, mule, or large dog, haunted solitary ways, and sometimes came upon belated travellers, as this horse was now coming upon me' (XII). Jane's imagination has been provided with some material, and it is not surprising, nor is it out of keeping with her character, as we know it, that the evening following Rochester's arrival at Thornfield, Jane is occupied in tracing in the clear embers of the schoolroom fire '. . . a view, not unlike a picture I remembered to have seen of the castle of Heidelberg, on the Rhine, when Mrs Fairfax came in, breaking up by her entrance the fiery mosaic I had been piecing together, and scattering too some heavy unwelcome thoughts that were beginning to throng on my solitude' (XIII). The rather strange owner of Thornfield, and the even stranger presence of Mrs Poole, are the subject of Jane's unwelcome thoughts, whilst the element of mystery, which seems to surround Thornfield, is the stimulus for the mental picture of the castle of Heidelberg, which is one of the most frequent subjects for etchings and, no doubt, had been seen by Jane in one of the books of illustration belonging to the Reeds. In fact, the castle at Heidelberg was one of the subjects of Turner's water colour paintings executed in 1844, but there is no evidence that Charlotte Brontë saw either the painting or an illustration of it, while writing *Jane Eyre*.

There is one other occasion when Jane resorts to day-dreams – this is after she has saved Rochester's life. After having put out the fire in Rochester's room, she returns to her bedroom, but she cannot sleep (XV):

> Till morning dawned I was tossed on a buoyant but unquiet sea, where billows of trouble rolled under surges of joy. I thought sometimes I saw beyond its wild waters a shore, sweet as the hills of Beulah; and now and then a freshening gale wakened by hope, bore my spirit triumphantly towards the bourne; but I could not reach it, even in fancy, – a counteracting breeze blew off the land, and continually drove me back.

What is significant in these three extracts is the change of personality which can be inferred from a study of the language and imagery used. The first passage suggests wish-fulfilment, in its lack of any clear-cut imagery, as references to 'bright visions' of 'incident, life, fire, and feeling' convey no particularity. In the second episode Charlotte Brontë has used the castle of Heidelberg as a symbol for Jane's thoughts about the recent mysterious events at Thornfield. In the third passage Charlotte Brontë uses imagery taken from nature, and in this instance, the sea and wind, which are used as metaphors for life and change respectively. This progression in the subtlety of writing in not fortuitous, but is a sign of the author's awareness of the changes taking place in the personality she is trying to describe, and purposefully choosing a method which will convey the changes of thought and feeling without explicit commentary. As soon as a relationship has been established between Jane and Rochester there are no further references to Jane's reveries, as life itself provides her with enough material to occupy her mind. In fact, her mind has so many new stimuli to assimilate that there are occasions when she resorts to dreams in order to clarify sub-consciously what her reason cannot disentangle. The first occasion that she dreams is after she has helped Rochester look after Mason, who has been injured by Bertha Rochester. The chapter in which Jane recalls the dream begins with a commentary on presentiments, signs and sympathies, and Jane tells the reader that she believes that such supra-rational experiences are possible, supporting her statement by recounting her dream of a child which '. . . failed not for seven successive nights to meet me the moment I entered the land of slumber' (XXI). To dream of a child is supposed to be a sign of trouble, and significantly a messenger arrives from the Reed household to tell her that John Reed is dead, and that Mrs Reed is dying, and has asked to see Jane Eyre.

The second occasion that Jane dreams is also during a difficult period: she is returning to Thornfield after her visit to the Reeds, and is uncertain as to how long she will be able to live there, as she has heard from Mrs Fairfax that Rochester has gone to London to make arrrangements for his wedding. On this occasion she dreams of '. . . Miss Ingram all the night: in a vivid morning dream I saw her closing the gates of Thornfield against me and pointing out another road; and Mr Rochester looked on with his arms folded – smiling sardonically, as it seemed, at both her and me' (XXII). This dream expresses a quite rational fear, as Jane has observed Blanche Ingram's efforts at singling out Rochester for her sole use. It also conveys the effect of this knowledge on Jane, by implicitly suggesting the deep emotional disturbance she experiences – through a dream. The night before her wedding day Jane has two dreams; she tells Rochester that, in the first instance (XXV):

I continued also the wish to be with you, and experienced a strange, regretful consciousness of some barrier dividing us. During all my first sleep I was following the windings of an unknown road; total obscurity environed me; rain pelted me; I was burdened with the charge of a little child: a very small creature, too young and feeble to walk, and which shivered in my cold arms and wailed piteously in my ear. I thought, sir, that you were on the road a long way before me; and I strained every nerve to

overtake you, and made effort on effort to utter your name and
entreat you to stop – but my movements were fettered; and my
voice still died away inarticulate; while you, I felt, withdrew
farther and farther every moment.

In the second dream she sees Thornfield Hall as a ruin; and she
is still carrying the unknown child in her arms. She hears the gallop
of a horse, which she is sure must be carrying Rochester away from
her; she describes her reactions (XXV):

I climbed the thin wall with frantic, perilous haste, eager to catch
one glimpse of you from the top: the stones rolled from under
my feet, the ivy branches I grasped gave way, the child clung
round my neck in terror, and almost strangled me: at last I
gained the summit. I saw you like a speck on a white track, les-
sening every moment. The blast blew so strong I could not stand.
I sat down on the narrow ledge; I hushed the scared infant in my
lap: you turned an angle of the road; I bent forward to take a
last look; the wall crumbled; I was shaken; the child rolled from
my knee, I lost my balance, fell, and woke.

When she wakens from the second dream it is to see a tall, large
woman with Jane's wedding veil on her head, which she afterwards
tears in two. That both dreams are prophetic is proved by subsequent events, and Charlotte Brontë's purpose in using this dream
sequence is, partially, to prepare the reader for the climax, but,
more significantly, the dreams suggest that subconsciously Jane is
aware of some barrier between herself and Rochester. One practical
impediment is Bertha, but she does not know that he is married;
what does worry her is Rochester's constant romanticising – calling
her an elf, a sprite, wishing to give her jewels and expensive clothes
– all of which she rejects, as she instinctively feels that he is trying
to escape from reality into a fantasy world. In fact, during the period
between their engagement and wedding Jane is constantly reminding
Rochester that she is not an angel, but an ordinary woman, who
has earned her keep by teaching, and that she is not beautiful.
Therefore, these dreams are not only prophetic, they also symbolise
differences in attitudes, which the previous chapter has shown up in
action. The fact that Charlotte Brontë has devoted a chapter to
dramatising the differences in attitude between Rochester and Jane,
and has also used the dream sequence, indicates that this is an
important point to the total plot of the novel, and shows the writer's
objectivity towards her subject matter. Charlotte Brontë is not
romancing, she is literally creating and forming, a work of art – the
novel *Jane Eyre*.

There are only two further occasions on which Jane dreams. The first dream occurs on the night of the disastrous and unconcluded marriage ceremony, when Jane knows that she must leave Rochester. In her dream she recalls her experience in the red room at Gateshead, and the moving light that had frightened her, which, in her dream, seemed to settle in the centre of the ceiling. She lifts up her head to look and sees (XXVII):

> . . . the roof resolved to clouds, high and dim; the gleam was such as the moon imparts to vapours she is about to sever. I watched her come – watched with the strangest anticipation; as though some word of doom were to be written on her disk. She broke forth as never moon yet burst from cloud: a hand first penetrated the sable folds and waved them away: then, not a moon, but a white human form shone in the azure, inclining a glorious brow earthward. It gazed and gazed on me. It spoke to my spirit: immeasurably distant was the tone, yet so near, it whispered in my heart – 'My daughter, flee temptation!'

To this Jane answers, ' "Mother, I will" '.

Charlotte Brontë's intention in using this dream is manifold, and the easiest manner whereby the meaning can be extracted is to take the symbols which she has made use of previously for expressing Jane's thoughts. The most obvious symbol to be found in this passage, and which was also used by Jane in the second picture she showed to Rochester, is the figure of a woman in the sky. In the picture it appeared to be unrelated to Jane but in the dream the figure communicates directly with her. The second symbol to be found in both passages is the moon, which Charlotte Brontë has used on numerous other occasions as an 'objective correlative' for a spiritual and true love. In the dream it illuminates the woman, so that Jane cannot help but comprehend what she wishes to tell her. The explicit meaning of the dream is clear, but what Charlotte also wished to convey, through metaphor and symbol, is that Jane must reject a love that is purely physical, because of its inherent inferiority to a completer love, which it is possible to attain. Therefore the function of the dream passage is to show that Jane's decision to leave Rochester is not a rejection of love, but the affirmation of the existence of a truer love. That Jane's feelings for Rochester are not transitory is confirmed by the following dream passage (XXXII):

> I used to rush into strange dreams at night: dreams many-coloured; agitated, full of the ideal, the stirring, the stormy – dreams where, amidst unusual scenes, charged with adventure, with agitating risk and romantic chance, I still again and again

met Mr Rochester, always at some exciting crisis; and then the sense of being in his arms, hearing his voice, meeting his eye, touching his hand and cheek, loving him, being loved by him – the hope of passing a lifetime at his side, would be renewed, with all its first force and fire. Then I awoke. Then I recalled where I was, and how situated [at Moor House – a school-mistress at the village school]. Then I rose up on my curtainless bed, trembling and quivering; and then the still, dark night witnessed the convulsion of despair and heard the burst of passion. By nine o'clock the next morning I was punctually opening the school; tranquil, settled, prepared for the steady duties of the day.

The passage confirms the depth of Jane's love for Rochester, and also shows that, however painful and disturbing it is for her to think about him, nevertheless he continues to be present in the subconscious part of her mind. Thus when Jane is confronted with the need to make a decision as to whether or not she should forget Rochester and become the wife of the missionary, St John, and asks for guidance from God as to what His will is, and the answer comes in the form of Rochester's voice calling her name, it is her intuition guided by some exterior force which makes her receptive to this phenomenon. She describes the experience (XXXV):

All the house was still; for I believe all, except St John and myself were now retired to rest. The one candle was dying out: the room was full of moonlight. My heart beat fast and thick: I heard its throb. Suddenly it stood still to an inexpressible feeling that thrilled it through, and passed at once to my head and extremities. The feeling was not like an electric shock; but it was quite as sharp, as strange, as startling: it acted on my senses as if their utmost activity hitherto had been but torpor; from which they were now summoned, and forced to wake. They rose expectant: eye and ear waited, while the flesh quivered on my bones. 'What have you heard? What do you see?' asked St John. I saw nothing: but I head a voice somewhere cry – 'Jane! Jane! Jane!' nothing more.

She takes heed of the voice, believing that it is not superstition, but the work of nature and, in her thanksgiving, she 'seemed to penetrate very near a Mighty Spirit; and my soul rushed out in gratitude at His feet'. Jane later learns from Rochester that on the same evening, at approximately the same time, he had called her name, and that he had heard her voice answering the call (XXXVII). Whether one believes in the existence of extrasensory perception or not is beside the point; what is important is to recognise the underlying significance of the voice episode for the depiction of character development and to the theme of the novel, as the voice symbolises the power of love to transcend time and space.

What the novel further asserts is that Romantic love is an element in true Christian love, and that it is natural to man to aspire to both the natural and the supernatural states of love. This is the point that Charlotte Brontë is establishing in the contrast between Helen Burns' life of Christian self-denial, and Jane's vehement claim for a Romantic life, and it is developed further in the Moor House section, when St John Rivers asks Jane to marry him, not for love, but to further the Christian faith. The fact that she refuses the offer is also important, as it affirms her belief that love and religion are compatible. If Jane had accepted St John it would have been an act of hypocrisy to her religion, and to her belief in Romantic love. It is when Jane has reached this state of human wisdom that she hears Rochester's voice calling her name.

What this analysis has shown, I hope, is that Charlotte Brontë's character portrayal of Jane shows a consistency in her depiction of Jane's predisposition to reverie and dreams culminating in her hearing the voice of Rochester. This suggests that Charlotte's imagination conceived the total personality of Jane, which her artistic talents embodied in the portrait of the complex and rounded character depicted in the novel. There are no passages in the novel which are an implausible or an improbable representation of innate character traits in Jane, nor are the actions described inconsistent with that character. Even the 'gothic' sections, the passages in which the mad wife and the strange Grace Poole are described, which most critics judge to be melodramatic and improbable, can be proved to be not only necessary for the working out of the plot and character, but a true description, without embellishment for the sake of sensation, of the conduct of persons whose minds and self-control have been destroyed by alcohol. The embarrassment of unsuitable marriage partners is as frequent now as it was in the 1840s: Thackeray had to face this difficulty, of which Charlotte Brontë was unaware when she dedicated the second edition of *Jane Eyre* to him, that his wife was mad, and had been placed in an institution. The fact that such circumstances occur in real life cannot be questioned, nor that it is necessary for Rochester to have a wife in name only, as otherwise an essential point about Jane Eyre's character could not be made, which is to show the evolution of a love that begins in propinquity and physical attraction, and develops into a mature love based on spiritual values, as well as on physical attraction.

Having established the need for such a moral complication between Jane and Rochester, which has to be resolved before their marriage can take place, it now has to be determined whether

Charlotte Brontë's depiction of Bertha was unjustifiably horrific, or necessary and accurate. In a letter to W. S. Williams, written in January 1848, a few months after the publication of *Jane Eyre*, Charlotte states (Shorter: 310-11):

> The character [of Bertha] is shocking, but I know that it is but too natural. There is a phase of insanity which may be called moral madness, in which all that is good or even human seems to disappear from the mind, and a fiend-nature replaces it. The sole aim and desire of the being thus possessed is to exasperate, or molest, to destroy, and preternatural ingenuity and energy are often exercised to that dreadful end. The aspect, in such cases, assimilates with the disposition – all seem demonised. It is true that profound pity ought to be the only sentiment elicited by the view of such degradation, and equally true is it that I have not sufficiently dwelt on that feeling: I have erred in making *horror* too predominant. Mrs Rochester, indeed, lived a sinful life before she was insane, but sin is itself a species of insanity – the truly good behold and compassionate it as such.

Charlotte Brontë did have first-hand knowledge of a fiend-spirit, as she was the unfortunate spectator of the moral and physical degeneration of her brother, Branwell, which began when he was dismissed from the Robinson household in 1845, and ended with his death in September 1848. There are many references, in Mrs Gaskell's *Life of Charlotte Brontë*, to letters written by Charlotte to her friend, Ellen Nussey, in which she says that owing to Branwell's conduct it is impossible to have any visitors at their house, but she omits giving a detailed description of his behaviour. However, John Lock, in his biography of the Rev. Patrick Brontë, gives some of the details omitted by Charlotte, which he has obtained from the diary of a Haworth parishioner, John Greenwood. Lock[6] states that on one occasion Branwell, in his comatose state, set his bed-clothes on fire, which his sister Emily extinguished by pouring pitchers of water over him. He also mentions the sordid physical deterioration that took place in Branwell; on one occasion his father found him lying in the churchyard and, at the age of seventy, he had to put his son over his shoulder, and carry him home. These events took place during the period that Charlotte was living at Haworth and while writing the novel *Jane Eyre*, which she began in August 1846, and completed in August 1847. Thus she had ample material to draw on for the delineation of the physical and moral degradation of a human being who has lost all self-respect through taking drugs and drink. It is surprising, therefore, that critics in general have not seen the substance of Bertha Mason's behaviour to be based on the

conduct of Branwell, though the French authors of a biography on
the Brontë sisters, M. & Mme Romieu, suggest that the characterisation of Bertha is based on the conduct and appearance of
Branwell.[7] They also claim that Charlotte witnessed Branwell's bed
being burnt. Mrs Q. D. Leavis also refers to the autobiographical
elements in the novel, in her Introduction to the Penguin edition
of *Jane Eyre*. However, most critics have tried to find resemblances
to her in Charlotte's Juvenilia creations. One such critic states
(Gérin: 334):

> Even her childhood story 'The Fairy Gift', written in 1830 when
> she was fourteen, contributed to *Jane Eyre*. In that story the hero
> who is given four wishes (and, characteristically, 'found the desire
> for beauty was uppermost in my mind. . . .') receives as his second
> wish a horrible wife, huge, brawny, and villainously strong, who
> attempts to strangle him and haunts the corridors and stairways
> of a great mansion in the true Bertha Mason style.

If Mrs Gérin's assumption is correct, that Charlotte Brontë used
material from her Juvenilia, which was pure romance, for her
mature works, which the writer explains as being based on fact and
the truth, then marks of such a transposition from romance to realism would show, as the transposed material would not naturally
arise from the exigencies of plot and character. I do not think that
this is evident: on the contrary, I believe that the mad Bertha
Mason is essential to the development of plot and character, acting
as a symbol and a constant reminder to Rochester of his past life,
which he tried to ignore when he attempted to marry Jane biga-
mously. The essence of the penultimate chapter is Rochester's remorse and repentance, and his wish for 'reconcilement with his
Maker', which a Christian believes it is never too late to effect, and
therefore, when he has reached this stage in his moral regeneration,
he is reunited with Jane. Mrs Gérin's assumption would not explain
the definite change that takes part in Rochester's character, and it
would make the presence of Adèle in the novel sheer extravaganza,
and not part of the moral burden which Rochester has put on his
own back, and which he must remove through his own effort. That
Charlotte Brontë accepted the Protestant belief in the burden of sin
and the individual responsibility for redemption is illustrated by her
references to Bunyan's *Pilgrim's Progress* in her novels and letters.

There are other indications of Charlotte Brontë's art as well. Mr
Martin, in *The Accents of Persuasion*, has commented on the 'black
pillar' simile used in describing Brocklehurst, and the 'marble'
rigidity and 'Grecian' perfection simile applied to St John Rivers.
To this could be added the movement of vision, from the descrip-

tions of the interior of houses, which predominate in the Gateshead and Lowood sections, to the opening up of the vista, by bringing in descriptions of landscape, in the Thornfield section, a change of perspective which symbolises Jane's developing personality. In other words, by giving the character a particular angle of vision at a particular period of her mental and emotional development, Charlotte Brontë has evolved a technique which more closely resembles the art of an impressionistic painter than that of a writer of prose. The sequential use of various visual images has already been demonstrated, which suggests that she has consciously developed an artistic form for the structure of the novel, which is unique and is not derived from the study of other novelists. That her creative powers, either intuitively or consciously, evolved a system of visual perspectives in order to portray the development in a character is also demonstrable in the opening up of the horizon, both metaphorically and literally, when Jane reaches Thornfield, and that this technique, which relies upon the perspective of the eye, has been derived from Charlotte Brontë's study of art is not improbable. In fact, we know that from an early age she thought of art as a profession for herself, and spent much time in copying mezzotints until her eyesight became affected (Gérin: 82). We also know that she attended the art classes of Mr William Robinson, which Mr Brontë arranged for his children. Furthermore, we are told by Mrs Gérin of the influence of art upon the Juvenilia writing, in particular the works of Mr John Martin, who was a frequent contributor to the 'Annuals', which the children read. She states (Gérin: 46):

> Any reader of Charlotte's and Branwell's earliest writings must be struck by the structural reality of their architectural descriptions, the recurring landscapes, the recognisable *landmarks*, that gives to the whole such an air of solidity and permanence, and is derived from the inspiration of Martin's pictures on their walls. [There were some of Martin's pictures hanging on the nursery wall.]

It is not surprising, therefore, that the mature writer continued to use techniques of presentation derived from her observation of the work of painters for the visual portrayal of growth in her characters. In fact, it is my conviction that Charlotte Brontë obtained her technique of multiple perspectives from a study of Turner's works, who we know was one of her favourite artists. In a letter to Miss Wooler, written in January 1850, she mentions that she had been taken to the National Gallery where she had seen Turner's paintings, and that this excursion gave her more pleasure than any of her other activities during her visit to London. This is not surprising as Turner was himself greatly influenced by Yorkshire scenery and, as a Yorkshirewoman, she would appreciate his interest in her part of the country. John Ruskin, commenting upon Turner's early style and the subject of his paintings, states that:

> I am in the habit of looking to the Yorkshire drawings as indicating one of the culminating points in Turner's career. In these he attained the highest degree of what he had up to that time attempted, namely, finish and quantity of form united with expression of atmosphere, and light without colour. His early drawings are singularly instructive in this definiteness and simplicity of aim. No complicated or brilliant colour is ever thought of in them; they are little more than exquisite studies in light and shade.[8]

The drawings to which Ruskin refers appeared partly in Dr T. D. Whitaker's *History of Richmondshire,* in 1823, and partly in *Picturesque Views in England and Wales,* published by Charles Heath in 1826, and both were studies of the English countryside done in mezzotints, a form of art that Charlotte Brontë had assiduously copied when she was a child. It is not surprising, therefore, taking into account her interest in art, and in Turner, that she should employ the 'definiteness and simplicity of aim' which is found in Turner's work, in her earliest novel, *The Professor,* which many critics have found to be a singularly dull book, because of its absence of colour and the simplicity of its subject matter and point of view. However, a unique method of presenting colour and perspective can be traced in Turner's later paintings, which I think is also present in *Jane Eyre.* Ruskin describes Turner's method in Volume I, *Modern Painters,* stating that:

> The comparison of Turner with Cuyp and Claude may sound strange to most ears; but this is chiefly because we are not in the habit of analysing and dwelling upon those difficult and daring passages of the modern master [Turner] which do not at first appeal to our ordinary notions of truth, owing to his habit of uniting two, three or even more separate tones in the same composition. In this also he strictly follows nature, for wherever climate changes, tone changes, and the climate changes with every 200 feet of elevation, so that the upper clouds are always different in tone from the lower ones; these from the rest of the landscape, and in all probability, some part of the horizon from the rest. And when nature allows this in a high degree, as in her most gorgeous effects she always will, she does not herself impress at once with intensity of tone, as in the deep and quiet yellows of a July evening, but rather with the magnificence and variety of

associated colour, in which, if we give time and attention to it, we shall gradually find the solemnity and depth of twenty tones instead of one. Now, in Turner's power of associating cold with warm light no one has ever approached or even ventured into the same field with him.[9]

We know that on the first occasion that Mrs Gaskell met Charlotte Brontë, at the Shuttleworth home in 1850, the latter expressed her appreciation of Ruskin's book on *Modern Painters*, and it is obvious, therefore, that she had read the work sometime between its publication in 1843 and the date of her meeting with Mrs Gaskell, and it is not improbable that the reading of the book had taken place during the period that she was writing *Jane Eyre*. At any rate, the dramatic possibilities that the use of colour can provide for a painting seem to have been recognised by Charlotte Brontë, because it is made significant use of in *Jane Eyre*. Each section of the novel has its overall tonal quality, beginning with the stark white and harsh red of the Gateshead section, symbolising Jane's desolation and passion, which merges into the greys and soft green and yellow of the Lowood section, when Jane begins to understand her nature, and to recognise her place in life. The Thornfield portion of the novel is presented in the strong colour of yellow, signifying midsummer in nature, and the midsummer of her emotional development, when she falls in love with Rochester. This is followed by another period of desolation in the Moor House section, which is depicted by a winter white of snow, and is further developed by the simile of St John Rivers, who is depicted as a block of 'white' marble. Then finally, in the Ferndean section, the predominating colours are of an autumnal dark grey and green, which reflect the chastened spirit of Rochester, as well as the restrained but true love of Jane for Rochester. Thus, within the novel, Charlotte Brontë has made use of the differing shades of colour which are to be found in nature, to indicate, metaphorically and dramatically, how these seasonal changes in nature correspond with human emotional and spiritual experiences.

Not only does she use colour for the presentation of experience, but the theory of perspectives which Turner applied to distinguish the different planes of vision in his pictures has also been adopted by Charlotte Brontë. This technique can be seen in the depiction of the extension of Jane's horizon from the Lowood section onwards, which truthfully presents Jane's view of her situation at that particular moment in time and, simultaneously, it suggests that it was a transitory impression, which was to be modified by later events. The following passage clearly illustrates this technique (XXV):

I sought the orchard: driven to its shelter by the wind, which all day had blown strong and full from the south; without, however, bringing a speck of rain. Instead of subsiding as night drew on, it seemed to augment its rush and deepen its roar: the trees blew steadfastly one way, never writhing round, and scarcely tossing back their boughs once in an hour; so continuous was the strain bending their branchy heads northward – the clouds drifted from pole to pole, fast following, mass on mass: no glimpse of blue sky had been visible that July day.

It was not without a certain wild pleasure I ran before the wind delivering my trouble of mind to the measureless air-torrent thundering through space. Descending the laurel-walk, I faced the wreck of the chestnut-tree; it stood up, black and riven: the trunk split down the centre, gasped ghastly. The cloven halves were not broken from each other, for the firm base and strong roots kept them unsundered below; though community of vitality was destroyed – the sap could flow no more: their great boughs on each side were dead, and next winter's tempests would be sure to fell one or both to earth: as yet, however, they might be said to form one tree – a ruin, but an entire ruin.

'You did right to hold fast to each other', I said: as if the monster splinters were living things, and could hear me. 'I think, scathed as you look, and charred and scorched, there must be a little sense of life in you yet; rising out of that adhesion of the faithful, honest roots. . . .' As I looked up at them, the moon appeared momentarily in that part of the sky which filled their fissure; her disk was blood-red and half overcast: she seemed to throw on me one bewildered, dreary glance, and buried herself again instantly in the deep drift of cloud. The wind fell, for a second, round Thornfield; but far away over wood and water, poured a wild, melancholy wail: it was sad to listen to, and I ran off again.

The first part of this passage consists of a generalised description of a stormy evening, of no special significance except that Nature's mood corresponds with Jane's feeling of apprehension, which is the result of her disquietening dreams of the previous night, and wakening up to find a strange figure of a woman in her room who tears her wedding veil. Having established the background tones, Charlotte Brontë draws the reader's attention to the stricken chestnut-tree, which would recall to mind the evening when Rochester had proposed to Jane – the same evening on which the tree was struck by lightning. Both these events are on a different time scale to Jane's present visit, as they belong to the past, and thus the tree clearly symbolises a significant event in Jane's life – her engagement to Rochester. Having established the focal point of the passage, we are told of the tree's present barren state, 'it stood up, black and riven', but the description does not end in the present, as the future is suggested in 'the little sense of life . . . rising out of the faithful adhesion of roots'. Thus the life of the tree is shown in its past, present and probable future state, which, as far as can be ascertained by the viewer at that time, is analogous to her own life – certainly of the past – and her apprehensive state of mind suggests that for the immediate present a similarity of situation is also possible.

This use of a multiple perspective, in which past, present and future are shown simultaneously from a contemporaneous point of view is an extremely complex technique, which it would have been difficult to express without the use of visual imagery. It can be assumed that Charlotte Brontë consciously used the tree as a metaphor for Jane's situation in life, because the narrative form of the novel is structured so that the entire story is told in retrospect by a thirty-year-old woman, and obviously only the places and events that were of significance to her would have been remembered after a time interval of more than ten years. The structure of the novel requires that there should be a presentation of the past historic view, and of the present, with a suggestion of a latent possibility for change in the future: this Charlotte Brontë has succeeded in conveying through the visual metaphor of the tree. In other words, she has made use of an impressionistic painter's technique of multiple perspectives in order to present past, present and future, and this technique resembles the work of Turner more than that of any other novelist or British artist.

To sum up the evidence obtained from this analysis: in *Jane Eyre* the author functions as the omniscient consciousness, controlling the pattern of the novel, but never intruding her point of view in it. Her craftsmanship is apparent from the manner in which she moulded this story, working from the appearance, thoughts and feelings of a ten-year-old girl to the conclusion, in which the mind, heart and soul of a thirty-year-old woman are presented. At each stage of the heroine's life Charlotte Brontë has selected the appropriate material for the depiction of the inner life of the character, which simultaneously portrays her outward actions. To do this she has made use of 'objective correlatives' selected from the artefacts of civilisation, i.e. books and paintings, and she has also used natural scenery. These 'objective correlatives' are used symbolically, allegorically or metaphorically, as the occasion demands and her artistic sensibility directs. She has also maintained a balance between her objective and subjective presentation of character, through the use of apostrophes to the reader, comments of other characters on the appearance and behaviour of the heroine, Jane Eyre, and mirror reflections. These three agents of the objective point of view are held in balance by the purely subjective phenomena of reveries, dreams and the voices, but with the mirror presenting both the objective and subjective views. Thus, throughout the novel, Charlotte Brontë is presenting two frames of reference, one depicting the inner life of the character, and the other depicting the external life of action. At no point are these two frames confused, although at the end of the novel they are united to form a single frame, in which the mature Jane Rochester is presented. Miss Millgate, in an interesting article on the narrative distance in *Jane Eyre*, comes to the same conclusion, but from a different approach. Her summing up expresses very concisely this unification. She states:

> Now, in the last chapter, the closing up of the gap between the narrator and the events narrated is coincident with, and dependent upon, a final integration of all aspects of Jane's personality. If there is, at this stage, no further mention of painting or drawing, that is because measurements of narrative involvement are no longer required, and, equally, because the aptitudes and impulses which Jane displayed in her pictures are now devoted not to compulsive self-expression, nor even to coolly objective portraiture, but to human communication of a peculiarly intense and passionate kind. To say that Jane Eyre, the heroine, merges at last with Jane Rochester, the narrator, is to make at one and the same time a statement about the novel's technique and about the novel's meaning. That this should be so is a high tribute to the sophistication of Charlotte Brontë's art.[10]

An art which is a perfect example of the Romantic style of writing, in which setting and scenery are used both factually and symbolically, and the character is portrayed from the core of the personality outwards, thus exposing the inner life of the soul and the workings of heart and mind, as well as the external stimuli which evoke these responses.

4 *Shirley*

Charlotte Brontë began writing the novel *Shirley* in 1847, shortly after the publication of *Jane Eyre*. There is no doubt that she had studied the criticisms on *Jane Eyre*, and intended to follow the critics' advice by making her third novel less melodramatic. She begins the novel with an apostrophe to the reader, in which she warns him against any expectations of that kind (I):

> If you think, from this prelude, that anything like a romance is preparing for you, reader, you never were more mistaken. Do you anticipate sentiment, and poetry, and reverie? Do you expect passion, and stimulus, and melodrama? Calm your expectations; reduce them to a lowly standard. Something real, cool, and solid, lies before you; something unromantic as Monday morning, when all who have work wake with the consciousness that they must rise and betake themselves thereto. It is not positively affirmed that you shall not have a taste of the exciting, perhaps towards the middle and close of the meal, but it is resolved that the first dish set upon the table shall be one that a Catholic – ay, even an Anglo-Catholic – might eat on Good Friday in Passion Week: it shall be cold lentils and vinegar without oil; it shall be unleavened bread with bitter herbs, and no roast lamb.

The setting for this 'something real, cool, and solid' is a cloth-manufacturing area in Yorkshire during the period of the Luddite riots in 1811/12. Against this background of social dissension Charlotte Brontë depicts the lives of people drawn from various social groups – clergymen and their curates, cloth manufacturers, landowners, spinsters, the factory workers and the unemployed, as well as two young ladies, Caroline Helstone and Shirley Keeldar, whose love-lives are affected by the current climate of social disturbance. Caroline Helstone's young man, Robert Moore, is too busy trying to rescue his mill from bankruptcy to spare much time for Caroline, and Louis Moore, his brother, who had been Shirley's tutor, is too embarrassed by the disparity of wealth between Shirley and himself to ask her to marry him. The romantic theme is the topic on which the novel concludes, but to read *Shirley* as a 'study of private emotion and thought in which the conflict is not primarily between master and men, Tory and Whig, but between the feminine viewpoint and the essentially masculine outlook of the world of commerce and politics',[1] is to ignore the obvious fact of the author's presence in the novel, and her chosen rôle, which is to present a chronicle of the times, in which the effect is shown of certain political and social phenomena on the lives of a few chosen individuals. All the characters are delineated with forceful personalities, and with the ability to think and speak intelligently on the topics which concern them. It is through Caroline's discussions with the Rev. Helstone, Robert Moore, Shirley and Mrs Pryor that Charlotte Brontë presents her ideas on the necessity of an education for women without wealth or marriage prospects, through the actions of the Rev. Hall and Miss Ainley that her ideas on a practical, practising Christianity are shown. Joe Scott and William Farren present the views of the factory workers and the poor; discussions between Mr Yorke and Robert Moore cover topical political questions on the Napoleonic war and the Orders-in-Council, and the current difficulties of cloth-manufacturers; and, finally, in the characters of the Revs. Helstone, Hall, and Boultby and their curates, we are given a picture of the differing interpretations of Christian ministry, and the attitude of the established church to the ministers representing the dissenting sects. In fact, a broad spectrum of English social history is covered in *Shirley*. In Mrs Gaskell's biography of Charlotte Brontë she explicitly states that (414-5):

> Miss Brontë took extreme pains with *Shirley*. She felt that the fame she had acquired imposed upon her a double responsibility. She tried to make her novel like a piece of actual life – feeling sure that if she but represented the product of personal experience and observation truly good would come out of it in the long run. She carefully studied the different reviews and criticisms that had appeared on *Jane Eyre*, in the hopes of extracting precepts and advice from which to profit.

From this evidence it is clear that Charlotte Brontë intended in her third novel to present a picture of life in a realistic setting of a specific place and verifiable time.

Professor Asa Briggs, in a paper delivered at a Brontë Society meeting in 1958, confirms the historical veracity of the events depicted in the novel, and mentions the similarity of character between the Rev. Helstone, of the novel, and a Rev. Robertson, of Heald's Hall, who was a friend of the Rev. Patrick Brontë. Furthermore, he mentions that local history records the Rev. Robertson as being a very militant clergyman, who actively helped the manufacturers who wanted to install machinery in their mills, and mentions a letter written by the Rev. Robertson to the owner of Rawfolds factory, which was situated within walking distance of Roe Head where Charlotte had attended school. In the letter to the owner, Mr Cartwright, the Rev. Robertson comments upon some of Cartwright's neighbours 'who are afraid they should be saddled with

great expense with these soldiers (Given the danger). I do not understand why they should think so'.[2] Mr Cartwright had foreign blood
in his veins, spoke French well, was tall and had dark eyes and
complexion, and lodged at his mill; thus in many respects he re-
sembled Robert Moore. On Charlotte Brontë's delineation of Moore
Professor Briggs comments that she '. . . was wise to distinguish between the courage of men like Moore and the supineness of the
manufacturers as a class . . .'. That the characters in the novel were
modelled on acquaintances known by Charlotte is corroborated by
Mrs Gaskell, who mentions that in *Shirley* (Gaskell: 413):

> . . . she took the idea of most of her characters from life, although
> the incidents and situations were, of course, fictitious. She thought
> that if these last were purely imaginary she might draw from the
> real without detection; but in this she was mistaken: her studies
> were too closely accurate. This occasionally led her into difficul-
> ties. People recognized themselves, or were recognized by others,
> in her graphic descriptions of their personal appearance, and
> modes of action and turns of thought, though they were placed
> in new positions, and figured away in scenes far different from
> those in which their actual life had been passed.

There can be no doubt then that the characters are 'real', but
that in itself would not necessarily be a mark of distinctive writing.
The distinction only arises when the inherent personality traits are
presented in such a manner that the thoughts and actions of that
person would appear to be entirely plausible in a given situation.
Charlotte Brontë took considerable care to ensure that the background details were accurate, which is proved by the known fact
that she studied the *Leeds Mercury* file on the Luddite riots for the
years 1812/14, but she would also have heard about this period of
local history from Miss Wooler, the principal of Roe Head, where
she was a pupil in 1831. Roe Head was situated in the midst of
the Luddite riot area, and the local inhabitants had many anecdotes
to relate about those times. Evidence that it was Charlotte Brontë's
intention to write on a topic of social history has been offered by the
late Miss Ivy Holgate, who mentions another interesting point with
regard to the preparation of *Shirley*. She states that in the course
of studying some documents belonging to a Mr Henry Speight, a
Yorkshire historian and author of the *Chronicles of Old Bingley*,
she came across an anecdote related to Mr Speight by a Mr Francis
Butterfield, who was living at Wilsden, not far from Haworth, and
who knew the Brontës. It appears that Charlotte Brontë visited Mr
Butterfield in the early part of 1848, in order to consult him about
the plot of a new novel she was planning to write; a novel which

was concerned with the Chartist agitations. However, Mr Butterfield dissuaded her from writing on that historical event, as he
thought it would be dangerous to express opinions on matters of
topical local industrial unrest at a time when there was much political upheaval, and, he added as a further argument, that it would
adversely affect her father in his relationship with his parishioners.[3]
Charlotte Brontë took his advice, and chose an earlier period of
Yorkshire history for the setting of *Shirley*. Thus it is obvious that
Charlotte Brontë took great care in her research of background
material, and that the *personae* of the novel are an accurate representation of Yorkshire character and speech. Furthermore, the
author is never absent from the novel – she is the observer and
recorder of the events. All these factors would seem to indicate that
Shirley should be read as a novel belonging to the genre of social
realism, and not judged as an unsuccessful novel written in the
romantic mode.

However, most critics have judged *Shirley* by the same standards
they applied to *Jane Eyre*. A contemporary critic, G. H. Lewes,
states that in his opinion (Allott: 165):

> . . . *Shirley* cannot be received as a work of art. It is not a picture;
> but a portfolio of random sketches for one or more pictures. The
> authoress never seems distinctly to have made up her mind as to
> what she was to do; whether to describe the habits and manners
> of Yorkshire and its social aspects in the days of King Lud, or to
> paint a character, or to tell a love story. All are by turns
> attempted and abandoned; and the book consequently moves
> slowly, and by starts – leaving behind it no distinct or satisfactory
> impression. Power is stamped on various parts of it; power un-
> mistakeable, but often misapplied. Currer Bell has much yet to
> learn, – and, especially, the discipline of her own tumultous
> energies.

This opinion has been reiterated by many modern critics, of whom
Laura L. Hinkley is a fair representative. Her comment on *Shirley*
is that it:

> . . . attempts enormously too much. *Shirley* concerns history,
> economics, ecclesiasticism, provincial society in its humours,
> stresses, and tragedies, personal fortunes of much variety and
> personal passions of great intensity, incessant exposition of char-
> acter, and the writer's own convictions and emotions. All these
> get horribly in each other's way. It is a wilderness in which the
> forest constantly disappears among the trees.[4]

There is one modern critic who diverges from mass opinion – Mr

Jacob Korg. In an interesting article, entitled 'The Problem of Unity in *Shirley*', Mr Korg suggests that in her third novel Charlotte Brontë tried:

> . . . to go outside the narrow interpersonal sphere of *Jane Eyre* and *Villette* and to apply the romantic myth to the world of social realities. When used as an instrument of criticism, her passionate belief in nature and individualism took the form of a peculiar religion. Drawn from a mystic source, the reveries in which Shirley and Caroline undergo the experience of communion with the absolute, it is extended into everyday life to provide standards of conduct.[5]

Although Mr Korg's language is somewhat obscure, he is trying to make a case for a different critical approach to this novel.

There is one other item of information with regard to the preparation of this novel which is important, as it indicates what was Charlotte Brontë's own idea as to the central theme of the novel. It is also the only novel with which she was at variance with her publishers over the title. Her original choice was *Hollow's Mill*, but her publishers, no doubt recalling the financial success of *Jane Eyre*, wanted the title to reflect the name of one of the two heroines; Charlotte recalls the occasion in a letter to W. S. Williams (Shorter: 165):

> If I remember rightly, my Cornhill critics objected to *Hollow's Mill*, nor do I now find it appropriate. It might rather be called *Fieldhead*, though I think *Shirley* would perhaps be the best title. *Shirley*, I fancy, has turned out the most prominent and peculiar character of the work.
> Cornhill may decide between *Fieldhead* and *Shirley*.

Charlotte Brontë's initial choice of *Hollow's Mill* suggests that she did not intend to write a biography of an individual, but desired to write a chronicle of events centred around a specific place, and for the place she chose Hollow's Mill, situating it in the Luddite riot area. Her alternative choice of *Fieldhead* would still reflect the name of a place, and not that of a person. In fact, by suggesting *Fieldhead* she has merely used for the title the name of the land of which Hollow's Mill is a part. In allowing the novel to be finally called *Shirley*, she still does not relinquish her central theme, as the title *Shirley* refers to the titular owner of Fieldhead, who was also the owner of the ground and buildings called Hollow's Mill. In fact, Charlotte Brontë was correct in her second choice of *Fieldhead*, as it is at Shirley's home that so many of the topics of current social concern are discussed and dealt with, for instance, the plans for the relief of the poor, and the right of women to choose their husbands.

If the novel is read as a realistic study of society, instead of assuming that it is another novel written in the romantic mode, then it will be found to have a coherence and order, in which character, event and action mutually support and illuminate two themes; these are class-relationships and feminism, the latter with its various related topics, such as the education of women, and freedom of choice in marriage. The most important of these, in terms of the number of characters involved, and the amount of attention given to the subject, is class-relationships, and the novel begins with a most satiric sketch of the three curates, Donne, Malone and Sweeting, who show their lack of Christian compassion towards their suffering parishioners, most of whom are factory hands employed at the local mills, and their lack of tolerance towards other religious sects at a tea-party which takes place at Donne's lodgings. Charlotte Brontë's description of the three curates is straightforwardly presented. She says (I):

> These gentlemen are in the bloom of youth; they possess all the activity of that interesting age – an activity which their moping old vicars would fain turn into the channel of their pastoral duties, often expressing a wish to see it extended in a diligent superintendence of the schools, and in frequent visits to the sick of their respective parishes. But the youthful Levites feel this to be dull work; they prefer lavishing their energies on a course of proceeding, which, though to other eyes it appear more heavy with ennui, more cursed with monotony, than the toil of the weaver at his loom, seems to yield them an unfailing supply of enjoyment and occupation.
> I allude to the rushing backwards and forwards, among themselves, to and from their respective lodgings; not a round – but a triangle of visits, which they keep up all the year through, in winter, spring, summer, and autumn. Season and weather make no difference; with unintelligible zeal they dare snow and hail, wind and rain, mire and dust, to go and dine or drink tea, or sup with each other. What attracts them it would be difficult to say. It is not friendship; for whenever they meet they quarrel. It is not religion; the thing is never named amongst them: theology they may discuss occasionally, but piety – never.

The negligence in fulfilling their pastoral duties – the accusation that Charlotte Brontë makes in this passage – is reprehensible at all times, but becomes even more censurable during times of economic duress, when the mutual interdependence between the classes, be it landlord and tenant, or manufacturer and labourer, or clergy and the poorer parishioner, is being challenged. Charlotte Brontë in her depiction of the clergy is supporting their work and recognises their function in society, but deplores the inadequacies of some of their members; hence the satire on the curates. That Charlotte Brontë refused to delete this chapter when requested to do so by her publisher, George Smith, is an indication of the importance this topic has to the theme of class-relationships in *Shirley*. In fact, she writes to Mr Smith, after the publication of the novel, telling him that at least one curate has changed for the better since reading *Shirley,* and that 'he has come to the house oftener than ever, and been remarkably meek and assiduous to please. Some people's natures are veritable enigmas: I quite expected to have had one good scene at least with him; but as yet nothing of the sort has occurred' (Gaskell: 451). From the tone of this letter it is obvious that Charlotte is pleased with the change in conduct that the reading of *Shirley* effected in one curate, at least. The fact that she mentions this event to Smith also suggests that she is tactfully telling him that her judgement is sounder than that of her publisher. It is a small example, but it corroborates my belief that to read Charlotte Brontë's novels accurately the critics should study what the author says, and not blindly follow the erroneous interpretations of past critics. But let us return to the theme of class-relationships, as Charlotte Brontë presents the subject in *Shirley*. All the characters in the novel are drawn into presenting different aspects of this problem, and each individual portrays a point of view which is logical in terms of his or her place in society, and plausible in terms of his or her personality. An examination of the Shirley Keeldar and Robert Moore relationship will show how Charlotte Brontë has used the theme of class-relationships as a centre around which the characters act out their designated rôles.

The relationship between Shirley Keeldar and Moore is that of landlord and tenant respectively, and we are told by Moore that it is only due to Shirley's financial help that his mill is able to continue operating after the frames were destroyed: an event which is described in the second chapter. Charlotte Brontë makes the point quite clearly that Shirley's rescue of Hollow's Mill is not undertaken because she is in love with its manager, but because she has a sense of social responsibility towards the local inhabitants, who would be absolutely destitute without their employment at the mill. This attribute of compassion for the poor is dealt with in great detail, and under Shirley's initiative all the other characters are forced to contribute to the cause which she has taken up. The chapter in which Charlotte Brontë describes Shirley's efforts at retrenching her domestic expenses, so that she will have some money to give to

the poor, and the later comical scene when the curate Donne comes
to visit her, but is frightened by her dog Tartar and hides in one
of the rooms upstairs, only make sense when they are read from
the thematic point of view. Shirley explains to Caroline, when the
latter finds her 'sitting gravely at her desk with an account-book, a
bundle of banknotes, and a well-filled purse before her', that she
feels responsible for the poor because of her social status in the
village (XIV):

> Yes; I feel of consequence. It is not an immense sum, but I feel
> responsible for its disposal; and really this responsibility weighs
> on my mind more heavily than I could have expected. They say
> that there are some families almost starving to death in Briar-
> field; some of my own cottagers are in wretched circumstances; I
> must and will help them.

To this Caroline replies:

> Some people say we shouldn't give alms to the poor, Shirley.

But Shirley emphatically states:

> They are great fools for their pains. For those who are not hungry,
> it is easy to palaver about the degradation of charity, and so on;
> but they forget the brevity of life, as well as its bitterness. We
> have none of us long to live: let us help each other through
> seasons of want and woe, as well as we can, without heeding in
> the least the scruples of vain philosophy.

By retrenching her household expenses Shirley is able to save £300,
and she uses this sum to head a subscription list to which the three
rectors, Hall, Helstone and Boultby also contribute. She then calls
a meeting at Fieldhead, at which are present the three rectors, as
well as Caroline, Mrs Pryor, and the Misses Hall and Ainley, to
draw up a list of needy parishioners – those who would spend the
gift judiciously.

Having established the importance of 'Captain' Keeldar's practical efforts at assisting the poor, the next chapter, in which the curates Sweeting, Donne and Malone come to Fieldhead to beg for a
donation for what *they* consider to be 'good' works, presents a con-
trasting point of view. From the dialogue between Donne and Shirley the reader can form his own opinion as to which of the two
speakers presents a truer form of Christianity. It is admittedly an
extremely satirical sketch of Donne, but it is also a revealing portrait of the obtuseness of some clergymen – a subject on which

Charlotte was well-informed. Donne explains the purpose of his visit to Shirley (XV):

> 'I came here this morning with a view to beg. . . . To beg of you a subscription to a school. I and Dr Boultby intend to erect one in the hamlet of Ecclefigg, which is under our vicarage of Whinbury. The Baptists have got possession of it: they have a chapel there, and we want to dispute the ground.'
> 'But I have nothing to do with Ecclefigg: I possess no property there.'
> 'What does that signify? You're a Churchwoman ain't you?'
> 'Admirable creature!' muttered Shirley under her breath:
> 'Exquisite address: fine style! What raptures he excites in me!' then aloud, 'I am a Churchwoman, certainly.'
> 'Then you can't refuse to contribute in this case. The population of Ecclefigg are a parcel of brutes – we want to civilize them.'
> 'Who is to be the missionary?'
> 'Myself, probably.'
> 'You won't fail through lack of sympathy with your flock.'
> 'I hope not – I expect success; but we must have money. There is the paper – pray give a handsome sum.'
> When asked for money, Shirley rarely held back. She put down her name for £5. After the £300 she had lately given, and the many smaller sums she was giving constantly, it was as much as she could at present afford. Donne looked at it, declared the subscription 'shabby', and clamorously demanded more.

If this passage is read as a development of points made in the first chapter, then it becomes clear that Charlotte Brontë has written this scene as a dramatic exposition of a religious stance which she abhors. Thus it will be found, as I hope to prove in the following pages, that the structure of *Shirley* is not haphazard when it is studied from the point of view of a thematic scheme, but that the novel would appear to be disjointed if read as a biography of a heroine who only appears in the eleventh chapter.

In fact, this scene has further ramifications, as the following discussion will endeavour to prove. Although it is doubtful whether Donne had any more success in civilising his hungry parishioners than he had in obtaining a large sum of money from Shirley, we do know that Shirley Keeldar's fund prospered, and that (XVI):

> By dint of Miss Keeldar's example, the three rectors' vigorous exertions, and the efficient though quiet aid of their spinster and spectacled lieutenants, Mary Ann Ainley and Margaret Hall, a handsome sum was raised: and this, being judiciously managed,

served for the present greatly to alleviate the distress of the unemployed poor. The neighbourhood seemed to grow calmer: for
a fortnight past no cloth had been destroyed; no outrage on mill
or mansion had been committed in the three parishes. Shirley
was sanguine that the evil she wished to avert was almost escaped;
that the threatened storm was passing over: with the approach
of summer she felt certain that trade would improve – it always
did; and then this weary war could not last for ever; peace must
return one day: with peace what an impulse would be given to
commerce!

Shirley's practical benevolence has not only saved lives, it has also
brought calm to a politically restive area. To enforce this point
even further, Miss Brontë gives the reader a description of the
annual Sunday School outing, at which all the participants appear
neatly and respectably dressed, commenting that (XVI):

Besides, the lady of the manor – that Shirley, now gazing with
pleasure on this well-dressed and happy-looking crowd – has
really done them good: her seasonable bounty consoled many a
poor family against the coming holiday, and supplied many a
child with a new frock or bonnet for the occasion; she knows it,
and is elate with the consciousness: glad that her money, example,
and influence have really – substantially – benefited those around
her.

It should be clear that Charlotte Brontë is not decrying the
Church, she is merely portraying the effect of practical Christianity
on a community, and her opinion is one held by a large number of
practising Christians, as a study of the history of the Evangelical
movement would prove. Indeed, there is a clergyman in the novel
who believes in practical Christian ministry; the Rev. Hall. That
the question of the clergy and their relationship to their parishioners was an important one is proved by the closing paragraph to
the chapter entitled 'Whitsuntide' (XVI):

It was a joyous scene, and a scene to do good: it was a day of
happiness for rich and poor: the work first of God, and then of
the clergy. Let England's priests have their due: they are a faulty
set in some respects, being only of common flesh and blood, like
us all, but the land would be badly off without them: Britain
would miss her church if that church fell. God save it! God also
reform it!

With this comment Charlotte Brontë closes the topic of the clergy, and their social, as well as religious, function in society.

Another aspect of class-relationships that Charlotte Brontë presents in scenes of characters-in-action, is that of labour relationships. This subject is dealt with fully and fairly, by using a diversity of characters to express their opinion, who are drawn from the two social groups concerned – that of employer and employee. I think, however, that it is Caroline Helstone who presents the writer's point of view on this topic, as early in the novel, in the chapter entitled 'Coriolanus', Caroline is depicted as trying to guide her lover Robert Moore to a more sympathetic understanding and treatment of his 'hands'. For this lesson Charlotte Brontë has Caroline making use of Shakespeare's play *Coriolanus* – a very clever choice, as the theme of the play is appropriate to Moore's situation, and, what is also important, in using a work of the greatest English playwright as an exemplum, she is sure of the approbation of her reader of the ideas presented in this play; this is a subtle rhetorical achievement, which would have been applauded by Puttenham, the Elizabethan rhetorician. The occasion is an evening at Hollow's Mill, and Caroline has persuaded Moore to read *Coriolanus* to herself and his sister. Charlotte describes the occasion (VI):

> The very first scene in 'Coriolanus' came with smart relish to his intellectual palate, and still as he read he warmed. He delivered the haughty speech of Caius Marcius to the starving citizens with unction; he did not say he thought his irrational pride right, but he seemed to feel it so. Caroline looked up at him with a singular smile.
>
> 'There's a vicious point hit already', she said: 'you sympathize with that proud patrician who does not sympathize with his famished fellow-men, and insults them: there, go on.'

By the end of the evening Caroline has applied the lesson of Coriolanus to Moore's life and conduct, and, by having got him to acknowledge that there is some similarity between himself and Coriolanus, she is able to say to him:

> I never wish you to lower yourself; but somehow, I cannot help thinking it unjust to include all poor working people under the general and insulting name of 'the mob', and continually to think of them and treat them haughtily.

Not only has Charlotte Brontë succeeded in dramatising her ideas on social philosophy, she has also succeeded in integrating the abstract subject matter with the personal interests of the two characters concerned, as Caroline is in love with Moore. Thus the scene is essential, both structurally and thematically, to the novel as a whole. The inclusion of the shooting incident, when Moore is injured by one of his hands, Michael Hartley, whom he persecuted for breaking his frames, is an illustration of the point that Caroline tried to make Moore understand when he read *Coriolanus:* that an employer who will have no 'truck' with his labourers, and who refers to them as 'the mob', is likely to engender a violent reaction from 'the mob'. Caroline's warning was not heeded by Moore, with the result that he was attacked.

In the final chapter entitled 'The Winding-up', in which all the social complications and personal misunderstandings are resolved, Charlotte Brontë, in an apostrophe to the reader, gives her opinion on this episode and on Moore's subsequent actions. She says (XXXVII):

I doubt not a justice-loving public will have remarked, ere this, that I have thus far shown a criminal remissness in pursuing, catching, and bringing to condign punishment the would-be assassin of Mr Robert Moore: here was a fine opening to lead my willing readers a dance, at once decorous and exciting: a dance of law and gospel, of the dungeon, the dock, and the 'dead thraw'. You might have liked it, reader, but I should not: I and my subject would presently have quarrelled, and then I should have broken down: I was happy to find that facts perfectly exonerated me from the attempt. The murderer was never punished; for the good reason that he was never caught; the result of the further circumstance that he was never pursued.

In this address Charlotte Brontë has brought together the theme of labour relationships and the theme of Christian charity, thus showing her power of narrative consistency.

There are many other passages in the novel in which Charlotte Brontë presents through her characters differing attitudes to class-relationships, so that the intelligent reader cannot fail to extract the point she is trying to make. Again, the choice of character through whom these ideas are presented is logical, and the delineation sustained throughout the novel. The labourer's point of view is best presented through the dialogue between William Farren and Shirley Keeldar, but before this scene takes place, Charlotte Brontë explains to the reader something of the nature and attitudes of the working classes, so that the reader is better equipped to understand the feelings behind the ideas expressed by Farren. She tells us that (XVIII):

Before gentlemen – such as Moore or Helstone, for instance –

William was often a little dogged; with proud or insolent ladies, too, he was quite unmanageable, sometimes very resentful; but he was most sensible of, most tractable to, good-humour and civility. His nature – a stubborn one – was repelled by inflexibility in other natures; for which reason, he had never been able to like his former master, Moore; and, unconscious of that gentleman's good opinion of himself, and of the service he had secretly rendered him in recommending him as gardener to Mr Yorke, and by this means to other families in the neighbourhood, he continued to harbour a grudge against his austerity. Latterly, he had often worked at Fieldhead; Miss Keeldar's frank, hospitable manners were perfectly charming to him. Caroline he had known from her childhood: unconsciously she was his idea of a lady. Her gentle mien, step, gestures, her grace of person and attire, moved some artist fibres about his peasant heart.

Having provided her reader with some background information as to the nature of the British working-class' attitudes to their superiors, particularly, their reaction to pride or insolence, Charlotte introduces William Farren in a dialogue between Shirley and himself, in which he tells her (XVIII):

'. . . I am varry well off. Since I got into t'gardening line, wi' Mr Yorke's help, and since Mr Hall (another o' t' raight sort) helped my wife to set up a bit of a shop, I've nought to complain of. My family has plenty to eat and plenty to wear: my pride makes me find means to save an odd pound now and then against rainy days; for I think I'd die afore I'd come to t' parish: and me and mine is content; but th' neighbours is poor yet: I see a great deal of distress.'
'And, consequently, there is still discontent, I suppose?' inquired Miss Keeldar.
'*Consequently* – ye say right – *consequently*. In course, starving folk cannot be satisfied or settled folk. The country's not in a safe condition; I'll say so mich!'
'But what can be done? What more can I do, for instance?'
'Do? – ye can do naught mich, poor young lass! Ye've gi'en your brass; ye've done well. If ye could transport your tenant, Mr Moore, to Botany Bay, ye'd happen do better. Folks hate him.'

Although this passage conveys the working-class point of view in a tone of rather acrid humour, nevertheless it enables the middle-class reader to understand that revolutionary or anarchistic ideas among labouring classes are not necessarily the result of a natural predisposition to hatred or envy of the upper classes, they may be a reaction against the intransigence and callousness of self-centred employers – like Robert Moore. Nor is Charlotte Brontë advocating anarchy by presenting only one side of the case. In the character of Mr Yorke, who is both manufacturer and land-owner, the reader meets a 'considerate and cordial' employer who, when it was necessary to dismiss an employee, 'would try to set them on to something else; or, if that was impossible, to help them to remove with their families to a district where work might possibly be had' (IV).

There are many passages in *Shirley* describing Moore's attitudes to his workers and theirs to him, and it is obvious that Charlotte Brontë did not include these scenes to fill out a rather thin love story; her intention was to present a novel of social realism to her reader, in which they could learn a little more about the lives of a group of people living in a rather remote region in west Yorkshire. It must not be forgotten that at the time that Charlotte Brontë was writing *Shirley*, contemporary writers like Mrs Gaskell and Dickens were also writing novels concerned with various strata in society, thereby hoping to broaden their readers' knowledge and understanding about other social groups, and that the mid-nineteenth century is recognised as being a particularly active period for social change. Contemporary with the publication of novels of social realism, current journals were discussing the Reform movement, Evangelicism, Chartism, and the Puseyite movement; thus *Shirley* conforms to the predominating style of creative writing of the mid-Victorian period, more so than *Jane Eyre* and *Villette*.

To say that the style of *Shirley* conforms to the genre of social realism novels does not imply that it is a better novel than *Jane Eyre* or *Villette,* but it does suggest that this novel should be read and judged from a different critical standpoint, one in which theme is recognised to predominate over the depiction of the inner life of the heroine, or heroines. If Charlotte Brontë's portrayal of Caroline Helstone is studied from the point of view of the theme of women's education, then the incident of her illness would be seen to be an explicable reaction to the drab future that lies before her, if she is not to be married. Having been introduced to Caroline in the fifth chapter, on the occasion when she spends an evening at Hollow's Mill, we are told that on the following morning Caroline questions her uncle as to why he is so scornful of marriage, and why he thinks people should not get married. This interest in the topic is due to her feeling of attachment to Robert Moore. Her uncle's reply that in his opinion the wisest action is to remain single, especially in the case of women, shocks her, but she pursues the subject further, asking him whether he thought that all marriages are unhappy. His answer is that ' "Millions of marriages are unhappy: if everybody confessed the truth, perhaps all are more or less so" ' (VII). After hearing this depressing statement, Caroline goes to see Robert again, expecting to get an affectionate reassurance from him, but finds instead that his conduct towards her is distant and most unlover-like. This experience, in conjunction with what her uncle has told her, has a profound effect on her spirits. It is after describing Caroline's experience that Charlotte Brontë addresses the reader in a lengthy comment on the situation of rejected women whose modesty forbids their asking for an explanation from the male as to why they are being treated in this distant and detached manner, because she is concerned about the difficulties under which women live, and wishes to advise her reader who may be confronted with a similar situation. She says (VII):

> . . . a lover feminine can say nothing; if she did, the result would be shame and anguish, inward remorse for self-treachery. Nature would brand such demonstration as a rebellion against her instincts, and would vindictively repay it afterwards by the thunderbolt of self-contempt smiting suddenly in secret. Take the matter as you find it: ask no questions; utter no remonstrances: it is your best wisdom. You expected bread, and you have got a stone; break your teeth on it, and don't shriek because the nerves are martyrized; do not doubt that your mental stomach – if you have such a thing – is strong as an ostrich's – the stone will digest. . . . For the whole remnant of your life, if you survive the test – some, it is said, die under it – you will be stronger, wiser, less sensitive.

Having prepared the reader for spinsterhood, it is not surprising that she depicts Caroline's thoughts to be following in that direction, because the 'condition of the single woman' is a subject which deeply concerns her, as a letter she wrote to William confirms (see Shorter: 352). Charlotte Brontë, through Caroline, makes the point quite clearly that she realises that Nature has assigned different rôles to men and women, a difference which society further re-inforces by erecting occupational barriers between the two sexes. This differentiation precludes the possibility of either sex understanding, or even being able to communicate freely with the other group. She deplores this dichotomy, as the rather strident tone of the latter portion of the passage indicates: 'break your teeth on it' is both a protest and an injunction. Nevertheless, the difference exists, and is presented in Caroline's observation that Robert's thoughts

> . . . were running in no familiar or kindly channel; that they were far away, not merely from her, but from all which she could comprehend, or in which she could sympathize. Nothing that they

had ever talked of together was now in his mind: he was rapt
from her by interests and responsibilities in which it was deemed
such as she could have no part (X).

Caroline's situation is typical of many young women, and what the
novel depicts is, firstly, the causes for unhappy marriages, which are
reflected in the history of Mrs Pryor's marriage. Secondly, there is
the effect of spinsterhood on women, and we are given a picture of
the lives of the Misses Ainley, Hall, Mann and Moore, who have
somehow found an answer to the question 'Where is my place in
the world?'. Thirdly, the novel portrays the possible alternatives
available to women who are unlikely to obtain husbands, and
Charlotte Brontë's remedy for this is to take up a profession. This
is why Caroline asks her uncle for permission to look for a place as
a governess, but only obtains a very scornful and untactful reply
from him (XI):

> Pooh! mere nonsense! I'll not hear of governessing. Don't men-
> tion it again. It is rather too feminine a fancy. I have finished
> breakfast, ring the bell: put all crotchets out of your head, and
> run away and amuse yourself.
> 'What with? My doll?' asked Caroline to herself as she quitted
> the room.

With no sympathy or help from her guardian, and having
observed the desolate lives of the Misses Ainley and Mann, and
experienced rejection by her lover, it is not surprising that
Caroline's spirits sink, and she becomes ill. It may be argued that
the chapter entitled 'Valley of the Shadow of Death' is a rather
exaggerated depiction of illness and mother love, but when one's
emotions are disturbed – as Caroline's undoubtedly were – then
one's reactions are in excess of normal rational behaviour. I think
that the title of the chapter gives us a clue as to how it should be
read, as it obviously refers to Bunyan's *Pilgrim's Progress*, to a
passage in which Christian has to combat the spectres of his imagination, and which has the same title. This episode in Bunyan's story
is taken by most critics to be an extended metaphor of a crisis point
in Christian's religious life, and I think that Charlotte Brontë
expected her reader to apply the same interpretation to her chapter,
by analogy. At any rate the emotional disturbance in the chapter
has been noted by many critics who judge it to be the ineffectually
disguised expression of the author's own desolation, as, during the
writing of *Shirley*, two of Charlotte's sisters, Emily and Anne, had
died. Mrs Gérin (390) comments:

Perhaps because it was so organically related to the circumstances of her life, *Shirley* achieved less artistic independence and wholeness than any of Charlotte's books. Its faults, however, are of construction, rather than content. For the same reasons that the plot was dislocated, the book contains some of the most philisophical thinking and the sheerest poetry of expression of all Charlotte's novels. The source of its inspiration – certainly as the tale progressed and death was the atmosphere it breathed – was more sustainedly spiritual than either *The Professor* or *Jane Eyre*.

The faults in construction which Mrs Gérin observes in *Shirley* are more probably due to the faulty premises upon which she has read the novel. Read as an exposition of the love lives of two young girls, Shirley and Caroline, perhaps this chapter is improbable. However, by changing the critical stance, and reading it as a social document, in which the effect of current attitudes towards women – the male attitude – is depicted, then the chapter describing Caroline's escape from society and its values into a psychosomatic illness is perfectly logical. The reader is told that she had a fever, the origin of which was unknown, but that she conjectured that (XXIV):

> Probably in her late walk home, some sweet, poisoned breeze, redolent of honeydew and miasma, had passed into her lungs and veins, and finding there already a fever of mental excitement, and a languor of long conflict and habitual sadness, had fanned the spark of flame, and left a well-lit fire behind it.

Caroline acknowledges that the spark was present prior to the onset of her illness, and her author, in giving the reader detailed examples of the events which have caused her 'mental excitement' and 'habitual sadness', has provided sufficient information to justify the nervous breakdown, which she here depicts. It is a warning to society that it should provide some form of interest or occupation to women who are debarred from matrimony, due to social causes which they cannot control. It must be remembered that after the Napoleonic war, the number of women of marriageable age in England was disproportionate to the number of men, the ratio being approximately that of five women to three men. Thus Charlotte Brontë's depiction of the 'never to be married' woman was a subject of topical interest.

Another aspect of the novel which critics have questioned is the accuracy of, and necessity for, delineating the at times aggressive masculinity in Shirley Keeldar's character. There are many passages in which Charlotte Brontë portrays Shirley as taking the initiative;

one has already been referred to when she initiates a programme of financial aid for the poor of the village, another is on the occasion of the Sunday school outing, when she is leading the group of children, and walking beside the Rev. Helstone. She finds the experience most exhilarating, as she confides to Caroline (XVII):

> I'll borrow of imagination what reality will not give me. We are not soldiers – bloodshed is not my desire; or if we are, we are soldiers of the Cross. Time has rolled back some hundreds of years, and we are bound on a pilgrimage to Palestine. But no, – that is too visionary. I need a sterner dream: we are Lowlanders of Scotland, following a covenanting captain up into the hills to hold a meeting out of reach of persecuting troopers. We know that battle may follow prayer; and, as we believe that in the worst issue of battle, heaven must be our reward, we are ready and willing to redden the peat-moss with our blood. That music stirs my soul; it wakens all my life; it makes my heart beat: not with its temperate daily pulse, but with a new, thrilling vigour. I almost long for danger; for a faith – a land – or, at least, a lover to defend.

The militant feminism which this passage depicts would, perhaps, be disturbing to Charlotte Brontë's male readers, but the fact that the ideas are not palatable is not an adequate reason for condemning the construction of the novel. What must be ascertained is whether there are exigencies in the structure of the novel, and in the depiction of the specific character, to warrant such a portrayal.

Shirley Keeldar is Charlotte Brontë's visualisation and illustration of the emancipated woman, the type of woman who has become the norm in the twentieth century. The portrait we are given is of a young woman, physically and mentally sound, who has independent means, and a tremendous amount of vitality to expend on living. She takes the initiative in social welfare work among her villagers; she lends Robert Moore money so that there will not be a greater number of unemployed at Briarfield, due to the failure of his mill; she loves action, and urges Caroline to go out late at night to see what the men are doing; she helps to care for the wounded soldiers after the Luddite attack on Moore's factory, and, not surprisingly, she has decided views as to whom she will marry. One can sum up all her actions as being characteristic of the 'emancipated' or 'liberated' woman. Despite these rather fearsome attributes, Charlotte Brontë, in her portrayal of Shirley, never allows her to become a prototype male. She is essentially female, and this quality in her personality is shown in those passages where her romantic sensibility is portrayed. One such passage occurs in the chapter following the introduction of Shirley to the story. She and Caroline have gone out for a morning's ramble, and characteristically the subject of love and marriage is discussed by them. Caroline comments that perhaps women would be happier if they made up their minds to remain single, and Shirley vigorously rejects that point of view, and tells Caroline that men (XII):

'. . . when they *are* good, they are the lords of čreation, – they are the sons of God. Moulded in their Maker's image, the minutest spark of His spirit lifts them almost above mortality. Indisputably, a great, good, handsome man is the first of created things.'
'Above us?'
'I would scorn to contend for empire with him, – I would scorn it. Shall my left hand dispute for precedence with my right? – shall my heart quarrel with my pulse? – shall my veins be jealous of the blood which fills them?'

The language in which Shirley expresses her ideas has the lyrical quality of the psalms, and, through its reference to the Genesis myth, the passage takes the reader back into pre-history, and beyond the then current attitude to male/female relationships, and thus establishes a historical basis for her ideas. Through Shirley, Charlotte Brontë seems to be making a plea for a new attitude towards women, in which they are accorded the equivalent status that the first woman in creation, Eve, had enjoyed; a status where women are regarded as worthy partners to their 'lords of creation', and not mental inferiors or merely bed-mates. The dialogue between Shirley and Caroline, after the school feast, only becomes clear when it is understood that Shirley's claim to direct kinship with ' "my mother Eve, in these days called Nature" ' (XVIII) is a reference to the time of creation when women were accorded co-equal status with men. It was at a later point in history that women were relegated to a lower sphere described in the novel as Milton's Eve. In *Shirley* we are presented with Charlotte Brontë's conception of the 'new Eve'. Thus the passage reflects a typical Romantic and Transcendental point of view, in which a spirit of wonder, a sense of potential greatness, and the mystery of creation is evoked. This Romantic philosophy is further developed in a passage which occurs after the Sunday school picnic, when Shirley refuses to go to Church, explaining to Caroline that she prefers to commune with her ' "mother Eve" '. Although Caroline admonishes her, Shirley is adamant in her belief that there is more spiritual truth to be found in Nature than within the stone walls of a building, and explains that to her Nature resembles the Eve ' "when she and Adam stood alone on earth" '. This highly Romantic statement provokes Caroline to ask

Shirley whether her vision of Eve is not Milton's vision of Eve, whch evokes the following reply (XVIII):

> Milton's Eve! Milton's Eve! I repeat. No, by the pure Mother of God, she is not! Cary, we are alone: we may speak what we think. Milton was great; but was he good? His brain was right; how was his heart? He saw heaven: he looked down on hell. He saw Satan, and Sin his daughter, and Death their horrible offspring. Angels serried before him their battalions: the long lines of adamantine shields flashed back on his blind eyeballs the unutterable splendour of heaven. Devils gathered their legions in his sight: their dim, discrowned and tarnished armies passed rank and file before him. Milton tried to see the first woman; but, Cary, he saw her not. . . .
> The first woman was heaven-born: vast was the heart whence gushed the well-spring of the blood of nations; and grand the undegenerate head where rested the consort-crown of creation.

These two examples, which have been selected from a number of passages in which a similar Romantic manifesto is presented, should vindicate Charlotte Brontë from the charge of having created an unfeminine woman in her delineation of the character of Shirley. Thus, when reading these passages from the point of view of the thematic development of the topic of women's emancipation, it will be found that not only do they occur at a dramatically significant and appropriate point of the story, but that Charlotte Brontë has created this character with a singleness of vision which is reflected in the unchanging values and actions upheld by Shirley throughout the novel. In the final chapter the author tells the reader of the difficulties Louis Moore experiences in getting Shirley to agree to a wedding date, although she has agreed to marry him, and that (XXXVII):

> It had needed a sort of tempest-shock to bring her to the point; but there she was at last, fettered to a fixed day: there she lay, conquered by love, and bound by a vow.

If this is read as the happy culmination of a simple love story, then Shirley's procrastination would appear to be an unnecessary and rather theatrical act of coquetry. However, it was not Charlotte Brontë's intention to write an ordinary love story; her purpose in the creation of the character of Shirley Keeldar was to present to her readers a woman who did not have to marry because she feared loneliness, or old age, but who married for one reason only, and that is love: Charlotte Brontë tells the reader that what finally conquered Shirley was love. This is a perfect example of a Romantic attitude, which becomes obvious when one studies the character of Shirley from the thematic point of view, and one bears in mind the rigid social conventions of Victorian England – its prudery – against which Charlotte Brontë had to contend, but which is obscured when Shirley's character is studied as a daguerreotype of the author's sister, Emily Brontë.

Thus, in *Shirley* Charlotte Brontë has depicted two heroines, who reflect, in their characters and actions, two of the major problems confronting women in the mid-nineteenth century. It is through Caroline Helstone that she expresses her ideas on the necessity for women's education, and here it might be apposite to mention that in 1847 the Governess' Benevolent Association started a scheme of training, and, at about the same time, Miss Murray, one of the Queen's maids of honour, collected funds for a women's college. These two schemes were combined, and led to the foundation of Queen's College, London.[6] Therefore, Caroline's predicament was a matter of topical concern at the time the novel was written. It was also a subject which engaged Miss Brontë's thoughts, as the following two letters to her friend Mr Williams show, both of which were written at the time she was engaged in writing *Shirley*. In the first letter, written in May 1848, she says (Shorter: 352):

I must, after all, add a morsel of paper, for I find, on glancing over yours, that I have forgotten to answer a question you ask respecting my next work. [*Shirley*] I have not therein so far treated of governesses, as I do not wish it to resemble its predecessor. I often wish to say something about the 'condition of women' question, but it is one respecting which so much 'cant' has been talked, that one feels a sort of repugnance to approach it. It is true enough that the present market for female labour is quite overstocked, but where or how could another be opened? Many say that the professions now filled only by men should be open to women also; but are not their present occupants and candidates more than numerous enough to answer every demand? Is there any room for female lawyers, female doctors, female engravers, for more female artists, more authoresses? One can see where the evil lies, but who can point out the remedy? When a woman has a little family to rear and educate and a household to conduct, her hands are full, her vocation is evident; when her destiny isolates her, I suppose she must do what she can, live as she can, complain as little, bear as much, work as well as possible. This is not high theory, but I believe it is sound practice, good to put into execution while philosophers and legislators ponder over the better ordering of the social system.

In the second letter, written in July 1849, she tells Williams that (Shorter: 367):

> Your daughters – no more than your sons – should not be a burden on your hands. Your daughters – as much as your sons – should aim at making their way honourably through life. Do not wish to keep them at home. Believe me, teachers may be hard-worked, ill-paid, and despised, but the girl who stays at home doing nothing is worse off than the hardest-wrought and worst-paid drudge of a school. Whenever I have seen, not merely in humble, but in affluent homes, families of daughters sitting waiting to be married, I have pitied them from my heart.

Through the depiction of Caroline's life Charlotte Brontë has presented, in a dramatic manner, her thoughts on this subject.

In the character of Shirley, Charlotte Brontë depicts the other important topic concerning 'the condition of women' question – the right for a woman to determine her own life, both in the public and in the private sphere. Of course, Charlotte is not the only novelist who has dealt with this subject. Jane Austen, in *Persuasion,* depicts Anne Elliot waiting for nearly ten years before Captain Wentworth, whom she loves, has achieved the financial stability and social position to satisfy her father, Sir Walter Elliot. What Charlotte Brontë contributes to the topic, through Shirley, is the Romantic vision of womanhood, which believes that only the highest kind of bond should exist between men and women – the bond of love – and this is precisely what Charlotte tells us exists between Shirley and Louis Moore. In fact, she even goes further and uses the expedient of Louis Moore's written confessions in his little black book to present a record of a conversation between himself and Shirley. Louis has told Shirley that he is leaving for America, but that he does not prize liberty as much as a loving wife, and explains what he means (XXXVI):

> I wish I could find such a one: pretty enough for me to love, with something of the mind and heart suited to my taste: not uneducated – honest and modest. I care nothing for attainments; but I would fain have the germ of those sweet natural powers which nothing acquired can rival: any temper Fate wills – I can manage the hottest. To such a creature as this, I should like to be first tutor and then husband. I would teach her my language, my habits, and my principles, and then I would reward her with my love.

What Charlotte Brontë has succeeded in doing in this passage is to present her ideas on the relationship that should exist between men and women in marriage, and, at the same time, she has made them relevant to the persons concerned. Louis Moore's statement that he would be 'first tutor and then husband', and that he would teach her his 'language', and then reward her with his love, is ambiguously phrased, as it both relates to the situation of the speaker and the auditor, and also reflects Charlotte Brontë's views on marriage in general, as her other novels show.

That Caroline and Shirley represent two distinct aspects of the general topic of the condition of women question is also made evident in the final chapter, in which the author describes the final stages of the Caroline Helstone and Robert Moore courtship, and also describes Louis Moore's difficulties in getting Shirley to agree to a wedding date. In the case of Robert and Caroline, she describes the social adjustments that will have to be made – Robert has to learn to accept a rather doting mother-in-law, and satisfy his future wife's social conscience that the money he will make will be partially spent on the improvement of local social amenities for his workers – hardly a romantic ending. However, in the final stages of the Louis Moore and Shirley Keeldar courtship Charlotte Brontë presents an illustration of the proverb that the course of true love never runs smoothly. We are told, through a conversation between Caroline and Robert (XXXVII):

> Shirley is as naughty as ever, Robert: she will neither say Yes nor No to any question put. She sits alone: I cannot tell whether she is melancholy or nonchalant: if you rouse her, or scold her, she gives you a look half wistful, half reckless, which sends you away as queer and crazed as herself. What Louis will make of her, I cannot tell: for my part, if I were a gentleman, I think I would not dare undertake her.

To which Robert replies:

> Never mind them: they were cut out for each other. Louis, strange to say, likes her all the better for these freaks: he will manage her, if anyone can. She tries him, however: he has had a stormy courtship for such a calm character; but you see it all ends in victory for him.

Thus, Louis Moore's love is tested by patience and understanding before he can claim the mastery over the woman he loves, and Charlotte Brontë has given the reader, in the depiction of their courtship, a picture of a pair of lovers who dramatise all the romantic notions that any reader of 'Currer Bell's' novels would expect, although she is not entirely successful in integrating these passages, which are rather too voluminous, with the main narrative form.

There are two modes of artistic expression which appear to be inappropriate to the novel of social realism. The first of these discordant elements is the use of the written form of confessional – the presentation of Louis Moore's thoughts and feelings through the medium of his writing in a little black book. Certainly, if the novel is read as another exercise in the style of *Jane Eyre,* then Charlotte Brontë's expedient of having Louis convey his thoughts and feelings in a diary is an awkward method, but if the novel is studied as a realistic picture of society at a given point in historical time, then some such enclosure and separation technique appears to me to be an acceptable method of distinguishing between the exterior actions of the character, and his interior feelings. There is no doubt that the passages which describe Louis Moore's entries in the diary are an inhibitory factor to the flow of the main events and themes, and perhaps they could have been omitted, or, at least, shortened. However, if they were left out, then the depiction of Romantic love, as represented by Shirley, would have been only a partial exposition of that topic. Thus the 'isolated' passages serve to make the distinction clear between the main narrative form and the parenthetical details provided in the diary entries. If this argument is accepted, then is can be claimed that in *Shirley,* Charlotte Brontë shows once again, a sensitivity towards truth to nature, though it does affect the artistic unity of the novel. The following quotation will, I hope, illustrate and explain the point I am trying to make. It occurs in the penultimate chapter, after Shirley has refused to marry either of her uncle Sympson's selected suitors, Mr Sam Wynne or Sir Philip Nunnely, and when Louis is no longer living at Fieldhead, but has come to spend an afternoon and evening there. He records the occasion (XXXVI):

I followed her into the drawing-room: Mrs Pryor and Caroline Helstone were both there: she has summoned them to bear her company awhile. In her white evening dress; with her long hair flowing full and wavy; with her noiseless step, her pale cheek, her eye full of night and lightning, she looked, I thought, spirit-like, – a thing made of an element, – the child of a breeze and a flame, – the daughter of ray and rain-drop, – a thing never to be overtaken, arrested, fixed. I wished I could avoid following her with my gaze, as she moved here and there, but it was impossible.

In reading this passage it must be remembered that Charlotte Brontë's objective in her portrayal of Shirley and Louis is to present a form of love which transcends the material plane of wealth and class, a love which has its origins in the spirit world, of which Nature is its tangible representative. Therefore, she has portrayed Shirley as the personification of nature, she is 'the child of a breeze and a flame – the daughter of ray and rain-drop'. To have allowed this heightened prose to appear without any separation from the main part of the narrative would have made her culpable of an error of artistic sensitivity and discrimination, and to have omitted it altogether would have been an act of untruthfulness to nature, and to her conception of Shirley's personality. Charlotte Brontë was aware that the metaphoric language which Louis uses when describing Shirley would have seemed incongruous, and therefore she anticipated and countered the objection by using the confessional form of a diary entry.

She was faced with a similar structural problem in the portrayal of the moment in timè when Shirley and Louis both realised that the feeling which existed between them was no longer that of master and pupil, but had developed into a profound feeling of love. To present this highly romantic moment in a novel which is essentially realistic posed some difficulty, which Charlotte Brontë resolved by having Louis Moore repeat verbatim an exercise that Shirley had written some years previously. Dr Duthie, who has studied the foreign vision of Charlotte Brontë, explains that:

> The strange *devoir* 'La Première Femme Savante', . . . expresses symbolically, in highly rhetorical language, originally French but translated into English, the ideal relationship of the sexes. In a primeval forest setting, the girl Eva becomes the bride of Genius, and so fulfils both her human destiny and the spiritual vocation of which she is intuitively conscious. The pantheistic tone of the essay recalls Emily Brontë, who helped to inspire the portrait of Shirley, and so does the implication of the title that 'the first bluestocking' was wise enough to confine herself to the school of Nature. But the atmosphere lacks the austerity of Emily's mysticism and is more suggestive of a Greek myth where gods descend to mortals. Genius is the bridegroom of Eva and the being who tells her: '. . . I take from thy vision, darkness: I loosen from thy faculties . . . . I claim as mine the lost atom of life. . . .' Translated into prose this expresses the relationship of Louis Moore and the brilliant Shirley . . . . In this context his social inferiority ceases to be important. He is the 'master' Shirley looks for in her lover, the 'man I shall feel is impossible not to love and very possible to fear.'[7]

By enclosing this description of romantic love within the framework of an exercise, Charlotte Brontë was able allegorically to represent the unique love that existed between Shirley and Louis, and to keep the heightened style separate from the main narrative. Her use of the expedient of Shirley's recitation of Bossuet's 'La Cheval Dompte', which is her acknowledgement that she is a willing victim, is stylistically in keeping with the previous exercise. On the use of this technique Dr Duthie comments:

> By a curious coincidence the mastering of a horse had already featured twice in the French passages transcribed by Charlotte Brontë, once when used by Bossuet as an illustration of his argument, and once when Buffon praised it as one of man's finest achievements. But both the seventeenth-century preacher and the eighteenth-century naturalist had thought of the process as a humane one – in the Romantic poem it becomes an image of violence, which retains its deliberate brutality in the translation. It conforms to another of the archtypal patterns of Charlotte's art, that of the victim, in this case a willing one, who is finally driven to breaking-point.[8]

It is the only example in her writing of the use of poetry as a metaphor for thought and feeling, and certainly it separates the Shirley/Louis love-story from the remainder of the novel.

The second inharmonious element in *Shirley* is the description of Martin Yorke and his act of chivalry towards Caroline. This episode begins with an account of his reading of a contraband volume of fairy tales, and describes a 'green-robed lady, on a snow-white palfrey', who is the subject of one of the tales, and 'a tall, pale thing, shaped like a man, but made of spray, transparent, tremulous, awful. It stands not alone: they are all human figures that wanton in the rocks – a crowd of foam-women – a band of white, evanescent Nereides', which forms the topic of the second story. At this point Caroline is introduced into the scene, and Martin teases her by telling her that Robert Moore is about to die. Caroline's reaction to this information arouses his curiosity, as (XXXII):

> In one sense it was, as he would have expressed it, 'nuts' to him to see this: it told him so much, and he was beginning to have a great relish for discovering secrets; in another sense, it reminded him of what he had once felt when he had heard a blackbird lamenting for her nestlings, which Matthew had crushed with a stone, and that was not a pleasant feeling.

What Charlotte Brontë is trying to convey in this passage is the stage of pubescence which Martin has reached, and to do this without giving offence to her perhaps prudish reader, she uses the stories that Martin is reading as metaphors for his nascent sexuality, which has been stimulated by the description of 'human figures that wanton in the rocks'. The arrival of Caroline at this point, whom he sees as the realisation of his sexual fantasies, causes him to impress himself on her sensibility in the only way that he knows will be effective – by telling her about Robert Moore. On seeing the effect of this news on Caroline, Martin is reminded of an occasion when he had seen a similar reaction to a break in a strong bond of attachment in nature, a bond which his brother had severed. Thus, he associates his recollection of what he has witnessed previously with the feeling that Caroline shows at the news, and this feeling of guilt corresponds to the inexpressible emotions that the reading of the contraband fairy tales has evoked in his mind, a mixture of curiosity, excitement and guilt. The portrayal of this adolescent experience is not essential to the main theme of *Shirley*, and one can only assume that Charlotte Brontë included this incident because she wished to portray the passionate aspect of a male/female relationship, of which her adult reader would have been aware, but which would have been inappropriate to the social themes with which this novel is concerned, as she explains in a letter to Ellen Nussey (Gaskell: 424):

You are not to suppose any of the characters in *Shirley* intended as literal portraits. It would not suit the rules of art, nor of my own feelings, to write in that style. We only suffer reality to *suggest*, never to *dictate*.

Although the various expedients that Martin invents in order to bring Caroline and Robert together are described with humour, these episodes are not relevant to the main plot. Thus, whereas it may be argued that the passages of Romantic prose which Louis Moore commits to his diary are thematically relevant, and have been adroitly separated from the main narrative, the same cannot be said of the Martin Yorke passages.

The most significant contemporary critic is G. H. Lewes, who states that *Shirley* is 'a portfolio of random sketches for one or more pictures', and it is certainly true that the delineation of the two characters, Caroline and Shirley, seems totally unrelated in the novel, if the novel is read as a biography of character. On the other hand, if the novel is read as a thematic portrayal of two kinds of love, then the presentation of 'prosaic' love through the character of Caroline, and 'romantic' love through the character of Shirley, will not seem inappropriate, particularly when we know that Charlotte herself was aware of the existence of differing forms of love. It is an interesting fact that in 1839 she wrote to a friend explaining why she could not accept an offer of marriage. She says (Gaskell: 169):

> Yet I had not, and could not have, that intense attachment which would make me willing to die for him; and if I ever marry it must be in that light of adoration that I will regard my husband. . . . I could not sit all day long making a grave face before my husband. I would laugh, and satirise and say whatever came into my head first. And if he were a clever man, and loved me, the whole world, weighed in the balance against his smallest wish, should be light as air.

This is the ideal of a romantic marriage, which she has transposed in *Shirley* into the delineation of the Shirley/Louis Moore relationship. On the other hand, a year later, Charlotte Brontë again wrote to a friend on the subject of marriage, when a completely different attitude is presented. She says (Gaskell: 193):

> Do not be over-persuaded to marry a man you can never respect – I do not say *love,* because, I think, if you can respect a person before marriage, moderate love at least will come after; and as to intense *passion,* I am convinced that that is no desirable feeling. In the first place, it seldom or never meets with a requittal; and, in the second place, if it did, the feeling would be only temporary: it would last the honeymoon, and then, perhaps, give place to disgust, or indifference, worse perhaps than disgust. Certainly this would be the case on the man's part; and on the woman's – God help her, if she is left to love passionately and alone.

The kind of marriage described in this passage, which is based on the mutual regard of two people for each other, is what she is presenting in the Caroline and Robert Moore union. Thus, in the portrayal of the topic of love, she is making a distinction between the needs and possibilities of differing personalities and the form of love which will be congenial to them, and she evolves a technique which, when the novel is read thematically, and the rationale behind it is understood, will be seen to be carefully formulated.

However, random portraiture is not the only criticism that Lewes makes with regard to *Shirley;* he also accuses the writer of incongruity of conception, and weakness of structure, and cites, as example, the section in which Robert Moore recounts to Yorke his unsuccessful offer of marriage to Shirley Keeldar, which Lewes thinks should have been presented dramatically (Allott: 169). If Charlotte Brontë had presented this event dramatically, then the only sensible and appropriate place for this would have been in Chapter XIII, where Caroline sees Robert and Shirley together, but does not hear their conversation. But, if Charlotte had followed Lewes' advice, and had depicted Caroline as being an auditory witness of the proposal of marriage, then her illness later could only have been interpreted as a decline due to a broken heart, which is not what Charlotte Brontë intended to portray. She wanted the reader to comprehend the problem of the unmarried woman who has no profession, and to understand that Caroline's illness is due to her general dissatisfaction with her situation in life, and not to her unrequited love. Furthermore, Chapter XXX, in which Moore's confession to Yorke about his disastrous proposal to Shirley is described, is important for the picture we are given of Moore's character, both its cupidity and pride, which we can expect from the 'Coriolanus' chapter onwards to be due for a tragic reversal. This also takes place in Chapter XXX when Moore is shot by Michael Hartley. Thematically, the passage is therefore more effective as Charlotte has presented it than it would have been if she had had the advantage of Lewes' assistance when writing the novel. It would seem, therefore, that Lewes' criticism is based on a faulty interpretation of the structure of the novel, and a misunderstanding as to the aim of the writer.

Throughout *Shirley* there are various levels of the comic presented. Some of it is pure burlesque, such as the description of Malone's vigil at Hollow's Mill the night the frames are destroyed, or Donne's visit to Fieldhead, or the scene with the irascible Mr Sympson; other passages are more restrained, but nevertheless expose the follies and foibles of the characters. The descriptions of Hortense Moore, Mrs Yorke, the Sunday school tea-party, and many more such passages, are written in an undertone of gentle satire, by a writer whose sense of the comic sees the incongruity of much of mankind's actions. This suggests that in *Shirley* Charlotte Brontë has made use of a different style of writing – which is true, she did write differently from the style of *Jane Eyre* because she had a different purpose in mind. Her purpose in *Shirley* was to present a chronicle of the lives of a group of people at a given period in history; planning that the novel should be a truthful and accurate depiction of real-life situations.

The evidence presented by this analysis can now be summed up. The major part of the novel is written in plain expository prose, in which the depiction of action predominates over the depiction of thought and feeling. However, there are the few passages of Romantic writing for which Charlotte Brontë has created an artificial frame, in the use of the diary, and the metaphoric use of poetry and fairy tale. Furthermore, there is another aspect of Romanticism to be found in *Shirley* which has not yet been discussed because it does not belong to the topic of the study, but which, nevertheless, is important to the understanding of the attitudes reflected in this novel.

In *Shirley* Charlotte Brontë is expressing a point of view which is radically individual, and different from the accepted norms of mid-Victorian society, her society. She is, firstly, making a plea for marriages to be consummated in love, and not through a dowry. Secondly, she is demanding that women be given an education to prepare them for a single life, if that is to be their fate. Thirdly, she is advocating a reform in the pastoral work of the church, and, finally, she is representing the apprehensions of the labouring class to the changes that the invention of machinery will bring to their lives. Her vision of man, and the society which he creates, is a Romantic one, because she believes that social systems and institutions are the tools given to man for the creation of his fuller life. In Charlotte Brontë's rejection of convention, and in her assertion of the rights of the individual, she is propagating a Romantic belief. Northrop Frye explains how Romantic ideas have affected literature, in a paper entitled 'The Drunken Boat: The Revolutionary Element in Romanticism'. He states:

What I see first of all in Romanticism is the effect of a profound change, not primarily in belief, but in the spatial projection of reality. This in turn leads to a different localizing of the various levels of reality. Such a change in the localizing of images is bound to be accompanied by, or even cause, changes in belief and attitude, and changes of the latter sort are exhibited by the Romantic poets.[9]

The change in the spatial projection of reality to which Frye refers, is the change from the fixed hierarchal pattern described in Genesis, in the creation myth, to a centre located in the consciousness of man: what exists is what he cognitively, intuitively and perceptually apprehends. It is Charlotte Brontë's conviction of the primary importance of the individual, which directs and controls her attitude to the social themes presented in *Shirley*, and which distinguishes her work from the contemporary novels belonging to the genre of social realism. In *Shirley*, Charlotte Brontë has written a Romantic manifesto, in which she pleads with society for a clearer understanding of the plight of the single woman, and greater compassion for the poor.

5 *Villette*

On a superficial reading of *Villette*, which is Charlotte Brontë's last completed novel, the reader might easily come to the conclusion that this novel is another work in the *Jane Eyre* style, as there are some similarities in the structure. It is written in the same autobiographical form, the events of the heroine's life being presented in a strict chronological order, and it is a love story. In fact, it differs radically in the style of the writing, being intentionally more restrained in expression, as it is infinitely more complex in meaning. The plot is simple, being the life story of a young orphan girl, Lucy Snowe, who goes to the continent after the death of her employer in England, and obtains a post as a teacher of English at a girls' school. She falls in love with the professor of literature, M. Paul Emanuel, who is drowned during a storm at sea, and the novel ends with Lucy established as the Directrice of the Externat that her lover has set up for her. The story covers fourteen years of Lucy's life, beginning when she is fourteen years old, and living in England, and ends in the town of Villette, when she is nearly twenty-eight years old. However, Charlotte Brontë has not set the story of Lucy's life in the immediate past, she has distanced it by imposing a time interval of approximately thirty years between the events described and the actual age of the narrator. Lucy tells the reader early in the novel that (V):

> Fifty miles were then a day's journey (for I speak of a time gone by: my hair, which, till a late period, withstood the frosts of time, lies now, at last white, under a white cap, like snow beneath snow).

The events which are recalled by the elderly narrator after such a long period of time, are obviously the occurrences which have had the greatest influence on her life, and they are described with the concreteness of vision appropriate to the present, which indicates the power of the experience on her mind, though the subdued language in which the events are described gives to the narrative a tone of acceptance and tranquillity – a stasis of the emotions. In fact the tonal quality of this novel has some similarity to Wordsworth's 'recollection in tranquillity' of those episodes in his past which have been influential on his later life.

Furthermore, there is another narrative technique which Charlotte Brontë, I think, successfully employs in her depiction of Lucy Snowe's life. She begins with an account of Lucy observing the actions of other persons, in which she personally is not involved but which will serve as a comparison for Lucy's behaviour when a similar situation occurs in which she is personally concerned. One such incident is the parting between Paulina and her father, of which Lucy gives an account (III):

> When the street-door closed, she dropped on her knees at a chair with a cry – 'Papa!'
> It was low and long; a sort of 'Why hast thou forsaken me?' During an ensuing space of some minutes, I perceived she endured agony. She went through, in that brief interval of her infant life, emotions such as some never feel; it was in her constitution: she would have more of such instants if she lived. Nobody spoke. Mrs Bretton, being a mother, shed a tear or two. Graham, who was writing, lifted up his eyes and gazed at her. I, Lucy Snowe, was calm.

This is the first description in the novel of a parting, and in Lucy's account of the episode the reader is made aware that Lucy is stoical by nature, and is, therefore, prepared for Lucy's attitude towards the departure of M. Paul. She relates (XLI):

> He deemed me born under his star: he seemed to have spread over me its beam like a banner. Once – unknown and unloved, I held him harsh and strange; the low stature, the wiry make, the angles, the darkness, the manner, displeased me. Now, penetrated with his influence, and living by his affection, having his worth by intellect, and his goodness by heart – I preferred him before all humanity.
> We parted: he gave me his pledge, and then his farewell. We parted: the next day – he sailed.

The suggestion of distaste towards the excess of emotion, conveyed in her attitude towards Paulina, prepares the reader for her show of self-control when parting with M. Paul. It is not that she feels the parting less; on the contrary, her statement of what M. Paul means to her is presented in absolute terms – he is 'preferred before all humanity' – but, by nature, she is not demonstrative. In a letter to W. S. Williams, Charlotte Brontë explains the type of character that she intended her heroine to have, and which is intimated in the name she chooses for her. She explains (Gaskell: 583):

> Unless I am mistaken the emotion of the book will be found to be kept throughout in tolerable subjection. As to the name of the heroine, I can hardly express what subtlety of thought made me decide upon giving her a cold name; but, at first, I called her

'Lucy Snowe' (spelt with an 'e'); which Snowe I afterwards changed to 'Frost'. Subsequently I rather regretted the change, and wished it 'Snowe' again. If not too late I should like the alteration to be made now throughout the MS. A *cold* name she must have; partly, perhaps, on the *'lucus a non lucendo'* principle – partly on that of the 'fitness of things', for she has about her an external coldness.

The narrative technique that Charlotte Brontë employs in *Villette* is to use certain key episodes in the early part of the novel as dramatisations of a human experience which Lucy is made to observe, and, from her comment on the event that she has observed, we can deduce what her attitude would be to a similar circumstance. The chapter which describes Lucy's last evening with Miss Marchmont would be superfluous if it did not have some analogous and metaphoric reference to Lucy's own life, and there are indications, in the resemblance of the language used to describe Miss Marchmont's death and that of M. Paul, that the early passage is intentionally included, because it is to be read as an analogy of Lucy's life after the death of M. Paul. Lucy recalls that on the evening of Miss Marchmont's death (IV):

> The wind was wailing at the windows; it had wailed all day; but, as night deepened, it took a new note – an accent keen, piercing almost articulate to the ear; a plaint, piteous and disconsolate to the nerves, trilled in every gust.
> 'Oh, hush! hush!' I said in my disturbed mind, dropping my work, and making a vain effort to stop my ears against that subtle, searching cry. I had heard that very voice ere this, and compulsory observation had forced on me a theory as to what it boded. Three times in the course of my life, events had taught me that these strange accents in the storm – this restless, hopeless cry – denote a coming state of the atmosphere unpropitious to life. . . . Hence, I inferred, arose the legend of the Banshee. I fancied, too, I had noticed – but was not philosopher enough to know whether there was any connection between the circumstances – that we often at the same time hear of disturbed volcanic action in distant parts of the world; of rivers suddenly rushing above their banks; and of strange high tides flowing furiously in on low sea-coasts. 'Our globe', I had said to myself, 'seems at such periods torn and disordered; the feeble amongst us wither in her distempered breath, rushing hot from steaming volcanoes.' I listened and trembled; Miss Marchmont slept.

The key image used to portray the advent of death is wind, which is also present when M. Paul's ship founders. The following passage describes Lucy's experience during the evening on which M. Paul's ship sinks and he is drowned (XLII):

> The skies hang full and dark – a wrack sails from the west; the clouds cast themselves into strange forms – arches and broad radiations; there rise resplendent mornings – glorious, royal, purple as monarch in his state; the heavens are one flame; so wild are they, they rival battle at its thickest – so bloody, they shame Victory in her pride. I know some signs of the sky; I have noted them ever since childhood. God watch that sail! Oh! guard it!
>
> The wind shifts to the west. Peace, peace, Banshee – 'keening' at every window! It will rise – it will swell – it shrieks out long: wander as I may through the house this night, I cannot lull the blast. The advancing hours make it strong: by midnight, all sleepless watchers hear and fear a wild south-west storm.
>
> That storm roared frenzied, for seven days. It did not cease till the Atlantic was strewn with wrecks: it did not lull until the deeps had gorged their full of sustenance. Not till the destroying angel of tempest had achieved his perfect work would he fold the wings whose waft was thunder – the tremor of whose plumes was storm.
>
> Peace, be still! Oh! a thousand weepers, praying in agony on waiting shores, listened for that voice, but it was not uttered – not uttered till, when the hush came, some could not feel it: till, when the sun returned, his light was night to some!

In both this passage and the previous one, Lucy alludes to the wailing of the wind as a herald of disaster; in both passages she refers to the Irish legend of the Banshee, a spirit whose wail portends death, and I think that Charlotte Brontë expected her reader to infer, from the explicitly stated fact of Miss Marchmont's death, that Paul Emanuel's life had ended during a storm at sea. Mrs Gaskell mentions an interesting point with regard to the ending of *Villette,* which supports this interpretation. She relates that Charlotte Brontë had told her (Gaskell: 582):

> . . . that Mr Brontë was anxious that her new tale should end well, as he disliked novels which left a melancholy impression upon the mind; and he requested her to make her hero and heroine (like the heroes and heroines in fairy tales) 'marry, and live very happily ever after'. But the idea of M. Paul Emanuel's death at sea was stamped on her imagination till it assumed the distinct force of reality, and she could no more alter her fictitious

ending than if they had been facts which she was relating. All she could do in compliance with her father's wish was so to veil the fate in oracular words as to leave it to the character and discernment of her readers to interpret her meaning.

If it is conceded that the description of Miss Marchmont's death is to be read as an analogue to the unstated death of M. Paul, then there is one interesting difference between the two passages, and that is in the language used. In the first passage, after describing the disturbing thoughts that have been brought to mind by the noise of the wind, Lucy objectively considers the phenomenon and considers the various natural calamities which can be expected to occur: epidemic diseases, erupting volcanoes, hurricanes, tornadoes. The tone of the passage is restrained, as Lucy's emotions are not deeply involved in Miss Marchmont's death. In the passage relating to M. Paul's death, however, the predominating tone is supplicatory; it is a plea to God to save her lover. It is also a desolate cry, as she knows from the signs in the sky, from the strange cloud formations, and her vision of the heavens, which are one flame 'so bloody, they shame Victory in her pride', that he will not be relinquished by the natural elements of disaster; his destiny is determined. The tone of the final sentence, with the suggestion of the utter stillness of the elements, and its reference to the absence of light for some, is of a depth of despair so great that one can almost sense the total suspension of life in the woman who watches and waits. The language of the passage is akin to the language of poetry; in its use of repetitive phrases, of alliteration, personification, metaphor and synecdoche. It indicates, in the density and variety of the modes of expression, as also in its tonal quality, the powerfulness of the emotions of the narrator, a quality of expression absent from the passage describing Miss Marchmont's death.

There is a further relevance between the chapter in which Lucy describes her conversation with Miss Marchmont, and the passage describing her feelings for M. Paul, which occurs at the end of the novel. Again, the reader is expected to see the analogy between the quality of Miss Marchmont's love and that of Lucy's, and to assume that Miss Marchmont's choice of spinsterhood will also be Lucy's. Miss Marchmont describes the quality of the love that she has known (IV):

While I loved, and while I was loved, what an existence I enjoyed! What a glorious year I can recall – how bright it comes back to me! What a living spring – what a warm, glad summer – what soft moonlight, silvering the autumn evenings – what strength of hope under the ice-bound waters and frost-hoar fields of that year's winter! Through that year my heart lived with Frank's heart. O my noble Frank – my faithful Frank – my *good* Frank! so much better than myself – his standard in all things so much higher! This I can now see and say: if few women have suffered as I did in his loss, few have enjoyed what I did in his love.

The love that Miss Marchmont describes is of a quality that is unique, and, therefore, she chooses to remain single when her lover is killed. At this stage Lucy is merely a sympathetic auditor, but she will recall the occasion and the sentiment described later in her own life. The passage in which Lucy describes her last evening with M. Paul, on the occasion when he offers her his love and asks her to one day share his life and to 'be my dearest, first on earth', is analogous in theme and sentiment to the passage describing Miss Marchmont's love, but again the language differs. Lucy narrates (XLI):

We walked back to the Rue Fossette by moonlight – such moonlight as fell on Eden – shining through the shades of the Great Garden, and haply gilding a path glorious for a step divine – a Presence nameless. Once in their lives some men and women go back to these first fresh days of our great Sire and Mother – taste that grand morning's dew – bathe in its sunrise.

The entire passage is an extended simile, in which the love of Lucy and Paul is claimed to be equal to the love of the first man and woman, who walked in Paradise. Again, Charlotte Brontë expects her reader to recognise that Lucy's love surpasses Miss Marchmont's, and to make the correct inference as to Lucy's future life after M. Paul dies. It is only out of deference to her father that Charlotte Brontë does not explicitly state that the elderly narrator has also chosen to remain a spinster.

It is the recognition of the complex structure of this novel, its nearly antiphonal balance between what the narrator observes and hears, and what she later experiences, that is a prerequisite to a correct understanding of what Charlotte Brontë was trying to express in *Villette*, in which the first four chapters are intended as an analogue of the final chapter. However, in the middle sections of the novel, those concerning her life in Villette, the transition of Lucy from an observer of life to that of a participant in it is stated without ambiguity, but the density of the language is maintained by a consistent use of symbolism throughout. The transition from a passive to an active rôle occurs on Mme Beck's fête day. The day begins with Lucy watching the preparations for the celebration; she describes the scene (XIV):

The whole day did I wander or sit there [in the garden] alone, finding warmth in the sun, shelter among the trees, and a sort of companionship in my own thoughts. I well remember that I exchanged but two sentences that day with any living being: not that I felt solitary; I was glad to be quiet. For a looker-on, it sufficed to pass through the rooms once or twice, observe what changes were being wrought, how a green-room and a dressing-room were being contrived, a little stage with scenery erected, how M. Paul Emanuel, in conjunction with Mademoiselle St. Pierre, was directing all, and how an eager band of pupils, amongst them Ginevra Fanshawe, were working gaily under his control.

She is interested to see how such an occasion is celebrated in a foreign country, but is glad that she is not called upon to take part in the festivities. Dramatically, that tranquillity is disturbed by M. Paul, who tells Lucy that she must take part in the play, owing to the indisposition of one of the pupils. He does not plead, he commands her to acquiesce – challenging the *'amour-propre'* of an Englishwoman to save the situation – a challenge which she accepts. Not only does she have to act the part of inane suitor for Ginevra's heart, whom she dislikes, but she is also required to assume male clothing, which is equally abhorrent to her. The description of her feelings after the performance is illuminating of the dormant propensities, which, till they are awakened by M. Paul, had lain hidden and undisturbed. She recalls those feelings (XIV):

What I felt that night, and what I did, I no more expected to feel and do, than to be lifted in a trance to the seventh heaven. Cold, reluctant, apprehensive, I had accepted a part to please another: ere long, warming, becoming interested, taking courage, I acted to please myself. Yet the next day, when I thought it over, I quite disapproved of these amateur performances; and though glad that I had obliged M. Paul, and tried my own strength for once, I took a firm resolution never to be drawn into a similar affair. A keen relish for dramatic expression had revealed itself as part of my nature; to cherish and exercise this newly-found faculty might gift me with a world of delight, but it would not do for a mere looker-on at life: the strength and longing must be put by; and I put them by, and fastened them in with the lock of a resolution which neither Time nor Temptation has since picked.

Lucy has experienced pleasure in being forced out of her customary passive rôle; and her resolution not 'to be drawn into a similar affair' is ambiguously phrased, as the final sentence implies that strength and longing are still alive, as the use of the present tense 'has' suggests, but that they are locked up, because neither 'Time' nor 'Temptation' has come again to break the lock after M. Paul's death. It is obvious that 'Time' refers to the interval between the present age of the narrator and the day M. Paul died, and 'Temptation' to the person who took her out of herself – M. Paul, whom she only knew for a year. Although Lucy resolves never to 'act' again, nevertheless, later that evening, she taunts Dr John about De Hamal, and is surprised at her temerity. She describes the occasion (XIV):

> For the second time that night I was going beyond myself – venturing out of what I looked on as my natural habits – speaking in an unpremeditated, impulsive strain, which startled me strangely when I halted to reflect. On rising that morning, had I anticipated that before night I should have acted the part of a gay lover in a vaudeville; and an hour after, frankly discussed with Dr John the question of his hapless suit, and rallied him on his illusions? I had no more presaged such feats than I had looked forward to an ascent in a balloon, or a voyage to Cape Horn.

Of course, what has transformed Lucy is the interest and attention she has received from a man – it is not yet love – from a man whom she finds provocative and stimulating. It is not surprising that, in the following chapter, we learn of Lucy's depression, which is brought on by the lack of activity, the distastefulness of her duties for the cretin, Marie Broc, and the absence of M. Paul, who has gone on a pilgrimage to Rome. Nor is it out of character for Lucy to go to a confessional, because the Catholic Church is her only link with M. Paul, the one person in a strange land who has taken her out of herself. The priest to whom she confesses offers her no spiritual comfort, because she is a Protestant. In fact, what he tells her is prophetic of her future destiny, and is also indicative of the forces which separate her from M. Paul. He tells her that (XV):

> Were you of our faith I should know what to say – a mind so tossed can find repose but in the bosom of retreat, and the punctual practice of piety. The world, it is well known, has no satisfaction for that class of natures. Holy men have bidden penitents like you to hasten their path upward by penance, self-denial, and difficult good works. Tears are given them here for meat and drink – bread of affliction and waters of affliction – their recompense comes hereafter. It is my own conviction that these impressions under which you are smarting are messengers from God

to bring you back to the true Church. You were made for our faith: depend upon it our faith alone could heal and help you – Protestantism is altogether too dry, cold, prosaic for you.

Père Silas's statement that Lucy would have to renounce her Protestant faith and become a Catholic in order to be saved is true, in the sense that because of her refusal to read the tracts M. Paul leaves in her desk, and her rejection of M. Paul's arguments against her faith, he is sent to Guadaloupe to prevent his marriage to Lucy. Thus, if she had become a Catholic then she would have been 'saved' by her marriage to M. Paul. Charlotte Brontë is suggesting, in the ending that she gives to the novel, that the religious differences between M. Paul and Lucy, although they personally transcend them, will not be condoned by society, and it is a religious society which destroys M. Paul. The final words that M. Paul speaks to Lucy are an implicit acknowledgement, and a recognition, of a love that transcends religious differences. He says (XLII):

Remain a Protestant. My little English Puritan, I love Protestantism in you. I own its severe charm. There is something in its ritual I cannot receive myself, but it is the sole creed for 'Lucy'.

I do not believe that the passages concerning Catholicism are extraneous to the main theme; on the contrary, I think the subject is central to the tragic love theme, which it was Charlotte Brontë's intention to portray in *Villette*. She chose to depict the lovers from opposing religious faiths, because she wished to assert the primacy of love over all religious, social or national differences, and to do this she had to establish the theme in a recognisable and accepted social context. What she is stating is that the power of love is greater than the power of the Church, that it is heaven created, as Lucy's description of their last evening together intimates, 'some men and women go back to these first fresh days of our Great Sire and Mother'. In this respect there is a resemblance between the theme of *Villette* and the theme of *Romeo and Juliet*. In both the novel and the play love is depicted as transcendental; as surmounting the obstacles that society creates. Its end is tragic, because society will never recognise such an instance of true love. Paul Emanuel is banished, and so is Romeo; they are victims and scapegoats of irreconcilable religious and social differences, and they are destroyed by their own society. In fact, Charlotte Brontë depicts Paul recognising the difference between the laws of God felt in a sincere heart, and the dogma of the Church, when he tells Lucy (XXXVI):

'Whatever say priests or controversialists', murmured M. Emanuel,

'God is good, and loves all the sincere. Believe, then, what you can; believe it as you can; one prayer, at least, we have in common; I also cry – "O Dieu, sois apaisé envers moi qui suis pécheur!"'

He leaned on the back of my chair. After some thought he again spoke:

'How seem in the eyes of that God who made all firmaments, from whose nostrils issued whatever of life is here, or in the stars shining yonder – how seem the differences of man? But as Time is not for God, nor Space, so neither is Measure, nor Comparison. We abase ourselves in our littleness, and we do right; yet it may be that the constancy of one heart, the truth and faith of one mind according to the light He has appointed, import as much to Him as the just motion of satellites about their planets, of planets about their suns, of suns around that mighty unseen centre incomprehensible, irrealisable, with strange mental effort only divined.

'God guide us all! God bless you, Lucy!'

If it is accepted that one of the underlying themes of *Villette* is Romantic love, then Charlotte Brontë's choice of a 'nun' figure, as a symbol for Lucy's emotional inhibitions towards the Catholic, M. Paul, is both subtle and appropriate. Yet one modern critic, Robert Heilman, refers to the 'neo-gothicisms' in *Villette*,[1] and another critic, Karl Kroeber, sees the 'nun' figure as a personification of a puritan quality within Lucy, which she destroys when she tears the nun's robes. His conclusion is that:

Although the nun motif in *Villette* is not faultlessly handled, it is an advance on the ironic manipulation of Gothic motifs in *Jane Eyre*. The theatrical fake Gothicism of the nun represents a true impulse in Lucy, whose temptation is to become cloistered (chapter 15) but whose destiny is self-dramatization, creation of self.[2]

To prove that these critics are not isolated in their point of view, I quote one other critic, Robert Colby, who states:

For *Villette* is most fruitfully approached as Charlotte Brontë's literary, not her literal, biography. Lucy Snowe's turbulent emotional experiences may be taken as an analogue of Charlotte Brontë's creative life, in that her achievement of mastery over her morbidly introverted imagination parallels Miss Brontë's own emancipation from the dream world she had envisaged in the Angrian legends of her youth. . . . While throughout the novel passion and rationality, art and nature, romance and reality continuously exert their rival claims on Lucy's imagination, in the end these tensions are resolved. Greater richness is produced also by the contrast between the tragedy of Lucy Snowe and the happier fates of the lesser heroines Polly Home and Ginerva Fanshawe.[3]

Other critics, both contemporary and modern, show even less understanding of the significance of the nun figure to Lucy Snowe's love story, as she does not represent sexual frigidity, but is used as a symbol for the barrier existing between Lucy and M. Paul.

It must be remembered that the character Charlotte Brontë is portraying is inhibited; by nature Lucy Stowe prefers to look on; it is Paul Emanuel who forces her to engage herself with life, and it is Paul who brings Lucy Dr John's letter, which is the inadvertent cause of her first vision of the nun. She goes to the attic because she wishes to read her letter undisturbed, but feels there are 'evil influences haunting the air', which materialise into an 'image like – A NUN' (XXII). Lucy drops her letter, and makes for the door to escape from the spectre. Dr John, who happens to be visiting Mme Beck that evening, finds the letter for her, and explains the phenomenon as 'a case of spectral illusion: I fear, following on and resulting from long-continued mental conflict' (XXII). To Lucy the apparition seemed real, which it was; in the person of De Hamal, who adopts the disguise of a nun so that he can visit Ginerva Fanshawe. However, there is another function given to the 'nun', which is to figuratively express certain as yet undefined, emotions in Lucy. To understand the symbolic meaning of the nun one must go back to the passage in which Lucy tells us about the legend. It appears that under a Methuselah of a pear tree there is a slab of stone, hard and black, which is 'the portal of a vault, imprisoning deep beneath that ground, on whose surface grass grew and flowers bloomed, the bones of a girl whom a monkish conclave of the drear middle ages had here buried alive for some sin against her vow' (XII). Although it is not explicitly stated, the primary vow which is required of a nun is the vow of chastity, and the dedication of her life to God, and presumably the nun had broken this vow, as the severity of the punishment would indicate. The legend also calls to mind the classical love story of Heloise and Abelard, who suffered a similar punishment for the same offence. Charlotte Brontë's purpose in using the nun legend is to symbolise Lucy's sexual awakening as well as her inhibitions, and to convey her awareness of the religious barriers between herself and M. Paul. It must be remembered that the first occasion that Lucy thinks about the nun is when she is forced by M. Paul to spend an afternoon in the attic to learn her part for the play. Lucy recalls the occasion (XIV):

I believe he did not know how unpleasant it was, or he never would have locked me in with so little ceremony. In this summer weather, it was hot as Africa; as in winter, it was always cold as Greenland. Boxes and lumber filled it; old dresses draped its unstained wall – cobwebs its unswept ceiling. Well was it known to be tenanted by rats, by black-beetles, and by cockroaches – nay, rumour affirmed that the ghostly nun of the garden had once been seen here.

Lucy does not see the nun on that occasion, because her feelings for M. Paul have not yet been aroused, but when he gives her Dr John's letter, with a taunting comment on its importance to her, she is aware that this little man is interested in her, that he will 'read the billet's tenor' in her eyes, as she is also aware of the fact that he is a Catholic and she is a Protestant, which would appear to be an unsurmountable barrier between the development of the natural feelings attracting them to each other. It is not illogical, therefore, that Charlotte Brontë has the 'nun' interrupting Lucy's reading of Dr John's letter, nor is the emphasis of the importance of the letter to Lucy fortuitous. In fact, there are two symbols being used simultaneously here. The 'nun' represents Lucy's feelings for M. Paul, and the letter her attachment to Dr John, and it is the importunity of the 'nun's' visit which disturbs her mental communion with Dr John.

The next occasion when Charlotte Brontë makes use of the 'nun' symbol is when Lucy erroneously thinks that the 'shape' gliding before her is the nun, but she soon realises that it is only Mme Beck, who is jealous of Lucy, and who imposes a constant surveillance on her. However, shortly after this, Lucy goes to the garret to fetch an evening dress, as she has been invited by Dr John to accompany him to the theatre. This time she sees a light 'like a star, but broader' (XXIII), which vanishes as she looks at it. This light symbolises an eventful meeting which will take place at the theatre, the effect of which will radically alter Lucy's life. She recalls (XXIII):

> That night was already marked in my book of life, not with white, but with a deep-red cross. But I had not done with it yet; and other memoranda were destined to be set down in characters of tint indelible.

In the rush of people making for the exits, a young girl is injured, who turns out to be Paulina Home de Bassompierre, and it is Dr John who protects Paulina from the crowd, and who gives her medical assistance later at her hotel. From the moment that Paulina and John resume a friendship which began when he was sixteen and she was six, Lucy no longer receives any letters from Dr John. In future, the recipient of his letters will be Paulina. We are told about this when Paulina consults Lucy about the propriety of accepting his letters (XXXII):

> 'Papa often lets me open the letter-bag and give him out the contents. One morning, about three weeks ago, you don't know how surprised I was to find, amongst a dozen letters for M. de Bassompierre, a note addressed to Miss de Bassompierre. I spied it at once, amidst all the rest; the handwriting was not strange; it attracted me directly. I was going to say "Papa, here is another letter from Dr Bretton"; but the "Miss" struck me mute. I actually never received a letter from a gentleman before'.

The communication of this news, figuratively speaking, puts out a light in Lucy's life, but it has not affected the 'nun' spectre. She will appear to Lucy again on the evening when she buries the four letters that she has received from Dr John, in a hollow near the root of the old pear tree. Lucy remarks that, in consigning her letters to the jurisdiction of 'Methuselah', she is not only 'going to hide a treasure', she also 'meant to bury a grief', her thoughts during this ceremony being disquietened. She relates (XXVI):

> If life be a war, it seemed my destiny to conduct it single-handed. I pondered now how to break up my winter-quarters – to leave an encampment where food and forage failed. Perhaps, to effect this change, another pitched battle must be fought with fortune; if so, I had a mind to the encounter: too poor to lose, God might destine me to gain. But what road was open? – what plan available?
> On this question I was still pausing, when the moon, so dim hitherto, seemed to shine out somewhat brighter: a ray gleamed even white before me, and a shadow became distinct and marked. I looked more narrowly, to make out the cause of this well-defined contrast appearing a little suddenly in the obscure alley: whiter and blacker it grew on my eye: it took shape with instantaneous transformation. I stood about three yards from a tall, sable-robed, snowy-veiled woman. Five minutes passed. I neither fled nor shrieked. She was there still. I spoke.
> 'Who are you? and why do you come to me?'
> She stood mute. She had no face – no features; all below her brow was masked with a white cloth; but she had eyes, and they viewed me.
> I felt, if not brave, yet a little desperate; and desperation will

often suffice to fill the post and do the work of courage. I advanced one step. I stretched out my hand, for I meant to touch her. She seemed to recede.

It is significant that Lucy does not run away from the apparition; on the contrary, for the first time in her life she challenges it. The change, from being a passive and fearful observer to actively engaging with the spectre, is a development in her personality, which her friendship with Paul Emanuel has brought about. However, as I have already stated, the 'nun' also symbolically represents Lucy's inhibitions, and the religious differences between M. Paul and herself, which she believes will be an impediment to real friendship, or to love; nevertheless, she is prepared to fight for friendship, and/or love, and challenges the 'nun'.

The last physical appearance of the 'nun' apparition in *Villette*, is when Lucy and M. Paul are together in the garden when he tells her that (XXXI):

I was conscious of rapport between you and myself. You are patient, and I am choleric; you are quiet and pale, and I am tanned and fiery; you are a strict Protestant, and I am a sort of lay Jesuit: but we are alike – there is an affinity between us. Do you see it, Mademoiselle, when you look in the glass? Do you observe that your forehead is shaped like mine – that your eyes are cut like mine? Do you hear that you have some of my tones of voice? Do you know that you have many of my looks? I perceive all this, and believe that you were born under my star. Yes, you were born under my star! Tremble! for where that is the case with mortals, the threads of their destinies are difficult to disentangle; knottings and catchings occur – sudden breaks leave damage in the web. But these 'impressions', as you say, with English caution. I, too, have had my 'impressions'.

The 'impressions', of which M. Paul speaks, are similar to Lucy's both in the literal sense, and in the figurative. It is at this point that they both hear a sound emanating from the old tree, which heralds the apparition. Lucy describes the occasion (XXXI):

A sudden bell rang in the house – the prayer-bell. Instantly into our alley there came, out of the berceau, an apparition, all black and white. With a sort of angry rush – close, close past our faces – swept swiftly the very NUN herself! Never had I seen her so clearly. She looked tall of stature, and fierce of gesture. As she went, the wind rose sobbing, the rain poured wild and cold; the whole night seemed to feel her.

The reason for Lucy 'never' before having seen the nun so clearly is, because up to this point, she was not sure of M. Paul's feelings towards her. Now, having heard, in unequivocal language, from M. Paul, of the existence of a natural affinity between them, she 'sees' clearly that the only obstacle barring their union is the Church. The spectre is comprehended, but not yet destroyed. The ritualistic destruction of the inhibitions will take place when she finds the nun's robes in her bed.

At this stage, Lucy does not know about the other 'nun' who haunts Paul Emanuel: a girl, Justine Marie, who became a nun when her parents refused to allow her to marry M. Paul, an event that had taken place twenty years ago. The Paul Emanuel aspect of the 'nun' motif is extremely ably presented in the chapter depicting Lucy's visit to the house of Mme Walravens, where she meets Père Silas, who personifies the religious barrier between herself and M. Paul, and from whom she learns of the history of Justine Marie, whose portrait hangs in the morning-room. She is painted wearing a nun's habit. Lucy now comprehends the nature and cause of M. Paul's 'morbid fancies', as she says (**XXXV**):

> Was I, then, to be frightened by Justine Marie? Was the picture of a pale dead nun to rise, an eternal barrier? And what of the charities which absorbed his worldly goods? What of his heart sworn to virginity?

The answer to the first of these questions is given later in the same chapter, when Lucy accepts the offer of friendship from Paul Emanuel. She describes the occasion:

> Yesterday, I could not have believed that earth held, or life afforded, moments like the few I was now passing. Countless times it had been my lot to watch apprehended sorrow close darkly in; but to see unhoped-for happiness take form, find place, and grow more real as the seconds sped, was indeed a new experience.
> 'Lucy', said M. Paul, speaking low and still holding my hand, 'did you see a picture in the boudoir of the old house?'
> 'I did; a picture painted on a panel'.
> 'The portrait of a nun?'
> 'Yes'.
> 'You heard her history?'
> 'Yes'.
> 'You remember what we saw that night in the berceau?'
> 'I shall never forget it'.
> 'You did not connect the two ideas; that would be folly?'
> 'I thought of the apparition when I saw the portrait', said I;

which was true enough.

'You did not, nor will you fancy', pursued he, 'that a saint in heaven perturbs herself with rivalries of earth? Protestants are rarely superstitious; these morbid fancies will not beset *you*?'

'I know not what to think of this matter; but I believe a perfectly natural solution of the seeming mystery will one day be arrived at.'

On Lucy Justine Marie can have no influence, but she does wonder whether 'the "morbid fancies", against which he warned me, wrought in his own brain'. The answer to this question, as well as to her uncertainties regarding M. Paul's moral obligations to Père Silas, Mme Walravens, and Mme Beck, is given to Lucy in the following chapter. The narrative technique which Charlotte Brontë employs to depict the forces against which Lucy has to contend is akin to the 'surrealism' of the painter. Lucy's description of the festival in the park has a phantasmagoric texture, which is partly due to the effect on her vision of the drug that Mme Beck has administered to her – inducing a state of excitement, instead of the expected stupor. It is also due to the fact that Lucy is observing the Père Silas group from a distance, and from a point of view which is radically opposed to that of the Labassecouriennes. Thirdly, the Père Silas group sees itself as having an 'in-sight' into a way of life from which Lucy is debarred. Fourthly, they are costumed actors taking part in a national festival. For the reader, the total effect is of a 'masque' being presented, with Lucy the Lady observing the Comus-like performance of the actors. Furthermore, the ironies inherent in the situation show up the distorted vision of all the characters present. The Silas party are celebrating the achievements of past heroes of Labassecour, little knowing that their most powerful enemy – in the person of Lucy – is still alive, and is present, watching them. Lucy is unaware that she will be confronted with a 'resurrected' Justine Marie, but she has a presentiment that this evening will be a revelation. What she sees when the awaited Justine Marie arrives is not the revivified nun of the picture, nor is it the nun of the garret, or berceau, it is a girl of Villette, well-nourished, fair, and fat of flesh. As she says (XXXIX):

So much for Justine Marie; so much for ghosts and mystery: not that this last was solved – this girl certainly is not my nun; what I saw in the garret and garden must have been taller by a span.

It is true that Justine Marie is not the nun, nevertheless she bears the same name as the girl to whom M. Paul had been affianced many years ago, and Lucy is made aware, when the girl joins the Père

Silas group, that their plan is for Justine Marie and M. Paul to marry. Lucy remarks 'the saintly consecration, the vow of constancy, that was forgotten: the blooming and charming Present prevailed over the Past; and, at length, his nun was indeed buried.' Lucy accepts the visual appearance of an intimacy between Justine Marie and M. Paul as being a true intimation of a forthcoming event, and admits to herself that this new-found knowledge has 'stripped away Falsehood, and Flattery, and Expectancy', and that now she is free. It is at this point that she decides to return to the pensionnat, and, on entering the dormitory, she finds (XXXIX):

. . . Stretched on the nineteen beds lay nineteen forms at full-length and motionless. On mine – the twentieth couch – nothing *ought* to have lain: I had left it void, and void should have found it. What, then, do I see between the half-drawn curtains? What dark, usurping shape, supine, long, and strange? . . .

My head reeled, for by the faint night-lamp I saw stretched on my bed the old phantom – the NUN.

A cry at this moment might have ruined me. Be the spectacle what it might, I could afford neither consternation, scream, nor swoon. Besides, I was not overcome. Tempered by late incidents, my nerves disdained hysteria. Warm from illuminations, and music, and thronging thousands, thoroughly lashed up by a new scourge, I defied spectra. In a moment, without exclamation, I had rushed on the haunted couch: nothing leaped out, or sprung, or stirred; all the movement was mine, so was all the life, the reality, the substance, the force; as my instinct felt. I tore her up – the incubus! I held her on high – the goblin! I shook her loose – the mystery! And down she fell – down all around me – down in shred and fragments – and I trod upon her.

This act of destruction of the nun's robes signifies, on the literal level, that there will be no further ghostly visitations, and, symbolically, it suggests that Lucy is now free from all fear, as she cannot hope for a future life with M. Paul, nor need she fear any meddling by the Church. The act of desecration of the robes is also a symbolic gesture conveying her realisation of M. Paul's release from the vow of celibacy, which she had previously thought to be an impediment to any serious relationship between them. She is free but desolate, as she does not expect to see M. Paul again. Charlotte Brontë's decision in the following two chapters to present the elucidation of a hitherto well-kept secret, and to depict the reversal of Lucy's previously held assumptions, is structurally and dramatically effective, as it brings together the literal and metaphorical aspects of the 'nun' theme. In Chapter XL we are told, in the form of a letter from Ginevra Fanshawe to Lucy, that the nun she had so frequently seen was none other than the Count de Hamal, who had used the disguise in order to visit Ginevra at the pensionnat: the mystery of the real nun was now resolved. In the following chapter (XLI) Lucy unexpectedly meets M. Paul again, and, despite the obstruction of Mme Beck, he takes her to a house which he has rented, and which bears a sign stating 'Externat de demoiselles. . . . Directrice, Mademoiselle Lucy Snowe.' This is the reason for his absence from the pensionnat for the past few weeks, and Lucy now realises that neither the power of the Church, nor the spectre of his past, both of which were symbolised by the nun, can intervene in their lives. The symbolic nun is also dead.

Thus, to have chosen a symbol, the 'nun', who personifies Lucy's sexual awakening, fears and religious doubts, and simultaneously, the 'past' of Paul Emanuel, and to have controlled the use of that symbol throughout the portion of the novel in which the fated love of Lucy and Paul Emanuel is depicted, is a fine example of the writer's mastery over narrative technique. To show the complexity and subtlety of Charlotte Brontë's writing, it has been necessary to discuss every reference to the 'nun' symbol in detail, and as the analysis proves, there are no inconsistencies or irrelevancies in the symbol used, both in its literal, and in its metaphoric sense.

The treatment of the Paulina and Dr John love theme in *Villette* has created some difficulty for many readers, who are confused when Lucy 'suddenly' transfers her affections from Dr John to give her attention to M. Paul. They infer that the poor health and loneliness of Charlotte Brontë had an effect on the structure of the novel, and that M. Héger, the director of the pensionnat in Brussels where she spent two years of her life, was the model of M. Paul. Mrs Gérin is the most lucid spokesman for this school of critics, and her considered opinion is that (Gérin: 494):

Though *Villette* marks the end of the road back from Brussels (it is Charlotte's noble valediction to her one-time 'Master') and was a book that could not have been written earlier, it was not merely a tale of experience past; it was, as a study of its plot and characters will reveal, an exploration of the present – a present so unpredictable that it left the author continually in suspense as to the issue. This uncertainty in Charlotte's actual circumstances and state of mind was the main reason why *Villette* proved so arduous a task.

Uncertainties and doubts no longer besieged Charlotte on the score of her feelings for Monsieur Héger. She had long recognized them for what they were – and hence the passionate righteousness of her retort to Harriet Martineau when accused of giving too

much prominence to the theme of love in the book: 'I know what *love* is as I understand it', she wrote Harriet in reply; 'and if man or woman should be ashamed of feeling such love, then there is nothing right, noble, faithful, truthful, unselfish in the earth, as I comprehend rectitude, nobleness, fidelity, truth and disinterestedness.'
What delayed the writing of *Villette* were the uncertainties and doubts immediately confronting her – the fearful problem of her solitude. . . .

Mrs Gérin is implying that Charlotte Brontë could not separate the problems of her own existence from the lives of the imaginary characters she depicts in *Villette*. I differ from that conclusion, as I believe that Charlotte Brontë, from the commencement of writing *Villette*, knew precisely the rôle each of the characters was to enact, but before I show the basis upon which my opinion is founded, I would like to quote from a letter which Charlotte Brontë wrote to George Smith, who was one of the first readers of *Villette*. The letter was written after she had submitted the manuscript of *Villette* to her publisher for his approval, but before it had been published. She replies to a criticism of Smith's (Gaskell: 587):

I must pronounce you right again, in your complaint of the transfer of interest in the third volume from one set of characters to another. It is not pleasant, and it will probably be found as unwelcome to the reader as it was, in a sense, compulsory upon the writer. The spirit of romance would have indicated another course, far more flowery and inviting; it would have fashioned a paramount hero, kept faithfully with him, and made him supremely worshipful; he should have [been] an idol, and not a mute, unresponding idol either; but this would have been unlike real life – inconsistent with truth – at variance with probability. I greatly apprehend, however, that the weakest character in the book is the one I aimed at making the most beautiful; and, if this be the case, the fault lies in its wanting the germ of the *real* – in its being purely imaginary. I felt that this character lacked substance; I fear that the reader will feel the same. Union with it resembles too much the fate of Ixion, who was mated with a cloud. The childhood of Paulina is, however, I think, pretty well imagined, but her. . . . (the remainder of this interesting sentence is torn off the letter).

In her reply to Smith Charlotte Brontë adroitly avoids giving a direct answer to his criticism of a change in direction from Dr John as a hero to M. Paul, although she admits that the weakest character in the novel is Paulina. Her comparison of Dr John's future married life with that of the legendary hero, Ixion, who was condemned to revolve eternally in Hades, is expressed ironically; however, it stresses the distinction she is making between Dr John's love and Lucy's. Although destiny will allow Dr John's love to be consummated in marriage, it is not comparable to the love between Lucy and M. Paul.

It has already been mentioned that there is a similarity between the tragic fate of Romeo and Juliet, and that of Lucy and M. Paul. However, it was not Charlotte Brontë's belief that this was the only possible fate for all lovers; it only applies to those who are so 'chosen' by destiny. A different destiny awaits the other characters, and this constitutes the second major theme upon which the delineation of all the characters portrayed in this novel is based.

To understand the principle determining Charlotte Brontë's portrayal of the Lucy and Dr John, and later, the Lucy and M. Paul attachments, one must comprehend the thematic patterns which, in *Villette*, govern the narrative patterns. There are two themes presented in this novel; firstly, the assertion of the existence of a transcendental kind of love; secondly, the belief that 'there is a divinity that shape our ends, rough hew them how we will'. The first of these two themes is only depicted in the Lucy—M. Paul relationship, the second governs the lives of all the characters, including Lucy and M. Paul. In fact, Lucy is the link between the two themes. The narrative pattern, which Charlotte Brontë has used for the depiction of the love between Lucy and Paul Emanuel, has already been discussed; it now remains to show the technique that Charlotte Brontë evolved for the depiction of the second theme. To portray the influence of destiny on the lives of human beings Charlotte Brontë has made use of two archetypal symbols – the 'sea' representing destiny, and the 'ship' standing for the soul of man. Furthermore, she suggests that the various manifestations of the 'sea' are the result of the intervention of a superior force – a divine spirit – who concerns Himself with the lives of His creatures. The first occasion when Charlotte Brontë makes use of these metaphors is in the chapter in which Lucy gives an account of the eight years of her life subsequent to her visit to the Bretton home. She states (IV):

> . . . I will permit the reader to picture me, for the next eight years, as a bark slumbering through halcyon weather, in a harbour still as glass – the steersman stretched on the little deck, his face up to heaven, his eyes closed: buried, if you will, in a long prayer. . . . Picture me then idle, basking, plump, and happy, stretched on a cushioned deck, warmed with constant sunshine, rocked by breezes indolently soft. However, it cannot be concealed that, in that case,

I must somehow have fallen overboard, or that there must have been a wreck at last. I too well remember a time – a long time – of cold, of danger, of contention. To this hour, when I have the nightmare, it repeats the rush and saltness of briny waves in my throat, and their icy pressure on my lungs. I even know there was a storm, and that not of one hour nor one day. For many days and nights neither sun nor stars appeared; we cast with our own hands the tacking out of the ship; a heavy tempest lay on us; all hope that we should be saved was taken away. In fine, the ship was lost, the crew perished.

Charlotte Brontë intimates that from early youth Lucy Snowe's 'ship' has experienced storms on the 'sea' of life. That this is not the fate of all people is suggested in the following passage, in which Lucy describes what she believes to be the divine pattern in the lives of Paulina and Dr John (XXXII):

Providence has protected and cultured you, not only for your own sake, but I believe for Graham's. His star, too, was fortunate: to develop fully the best of his nature, a companion like you was needed: there you are, ready. You must be united. I knew it the first day I saw you together at La Terrasse. In all that mutually concerns you and Graham there seems to me promise, plan, harmony. I do not think the sunny youth of either will prove the forerunner of stormy age. I think it is deemed good that you two should live in peace and be happy – not as angels, but as few are happy amongst mortals. Some lives *are* thus blessed; it is God's will: it is the attesting trace and lingering evidence of Eden. Other lives run from the first another course. Other travellers encounter weather fitful and gusty, wild and variable – breast adverse winds, are belated and overtaken by the early closing winter night. Neither can this happen without the sanction of God; and I know that, amidst His boundless works, is somewhere stored the secret of this last fate's justice: I know that His treasures contain the proof as the promise of its mercy.'

Thus, a clear distinction is made between the storm-free vessel carrying Paulina and Dr John, and the vessel which takes Lucy on her life's journey. She believes that her 'ship' is charted by Providence to sail on a storm-tossed sea; and, to complete the symbol, Charlotte Brontë devises the novel to end with the loss of Paul Emanuel's life at 'sea'. This conviction in destiny governing human lives is not an idea which suddenly occurred to Charlotte Brontë during the course of writing *Villette;* on the contrary, it was a conviction she held prior to writing the novel, and which governed her planning of its structure. The evidence for this statement is to be found in a letter she wrote to George Smith, in which she tells him that (Gaskell: 581-2):

> Most of the third volume is given to the development of the 'crabbed Professor's' character. Lucy must not marry Dr John; he is far too youthful, handsome, bright-spirited, and sweet-tempered; he is a 'curled darling' of Nature and of Fortune, and must draw a prize in life's lottery. His wife must be young, rich, pretty; he must be made very happy indeed. If Lucy marries anybody it must be the Professor – a man in whom there is much to forgive, much to 'put up with'. But I am not leniently disposed towards Miss *Frost:* from the beginning I never meant to appoint her lines in pleasant places.

One must accept the author's statement, but the critic has the right to examine the work in question to see if the idea has been successfully transposed on to the creation. Certainly, in the character portrayal of Paulina, I think that Charlotte Brontë has successfully conveyed a picture of a life that will sail on sunny seas. Furthermore, there is Lucy's prophesy to Paulina to support our impression, which has already been quoted: see page 118. However, in those passages in which Lucy's relationship with Dr John is described, the reader is not so sure of what impression to form about his character. Lucy gives us two pictures – a public view and a private view, and insists that they are both correct. The public view is of a man who is kind and attractive, appreciative of beauty, interested in the arts, and a dedicated doctor. The private view is of a man who takes an inordinately long time to discover the true nature of Ginevra Fanshawe, and who seems to obtain some sort of personal gratification from Lucy's, as well as Paulina's adoration for him. It is Lucy who gives us a sketch of his personality (XIX):

> Human fallibility leavened him throughout: there was no hour, and scarcely a moment of time I spent with him, that in act, or speech, or look, he did not betray something that was not of a god. A god could not have the cruel vanity of Dr John, nor his sometime levity. No immortal could have resembled him in his occasional temporary oblivion of all but the present – in his passing passion for that present; shown not coarsely, by devoting it to material indulgence, but selfishly, by extracting from it whatever it could yield of nutriment to his masculine self-love: his delight was to feed that ravenous sentiment, without thought of the price of provender, or care for the cost of keeping it sleek and high-pampered.

A picture of a vain, but successful, man. One can understand
Lucy's acidulous description of him; she knows the true nature of
Ginevra, and she is irritated at his lack of reliance upon her judgement. However, her reaction to the termination of his correspondence would seem to be at variance with the above sentiment, unless
it is read as the expression of Lucy's subjective point of view, for
whom Dr John's letters have been an assuagement for her 'love-
parched' existence. In fact, her description of the effect of his silence
confirms the latter interpretation. She states (XXVI):

> That goodly river on whose banks I had sojourned, of whose
> waves a few reviving drops had trickled to my lips, was bending
> to another course: it was leaving my little hut and field forlorn
> and sand-dry, pouring its wealth of waters far away. The change
> was right, just, natural; not a word could be said: but I loved my
> Rhine, my Nile; I had almost worshipped my Ganges, and I
> grieved that the grand tide should roll estranged, should vanish
> like a false mirage. Though stoical, I was not quite a stoic; drops
> streamed fast on my hands, on my desk: I wept one sultry shower,
> heavy and brief.

The imagery used in this passage clearly evokes the differences in
character between Dr John and Lucy. The former is blessed with
an abundance of wealth and the promise of an exciting future, the
other is doomed to live poorly, and to struggle to obtain sufficient
sustenance for body and soul. They would not be a successful match.
There is one more picture that we are given of Dr John. At the
fête, while Lucy is observing the Père Silas party, she suddenly
notices that Dr John has recognised her. By a gesture she indicates
that she does not want her presence to be known by the others, and
Dr John respects her plea. She comments (XXXVIII):

> He resumed his seat, nor did he again turn or disturb me by a
> glance, except indeed for one single instant, when a look, rather
> solicitous than curious, stole my way – speaking what somehow
> stilled my heart like 'the south wind quieting the earth'. Graham's
> thoughts of me were not entirely those of a frozen indifference,
> after all. I believe in that goodly mansion, his heart, he kept one
> little place under the skylights where Lucy might have entertain-
> ment, if she chose to call. It was not so handsome as the chambers
> where he lodged his male friends; it was not like the hall where
> he accommodated his philanthropy, or the library where he
> treasured his science, still less did it resemble the pavilion where
> his marriage feast was splendidly spread; yet, gradually, by long

and equal kindness, he proved to me that he kept one little closet, over the door of which was written 'Lucy's Room'. I kept a place for him, too – a place of which I never took the measure, either by rule or compass: I think it was like the tent of Peri-Banou. All my life long I carried it folded in the hollow of my hand – yet, released from that hold and constriction, I know not but its innate capacity for expanse might have magnified it into a tabernacle for a host.

The simile she uses to indicate her place in Graham's life is of a small place – a sky-light – to which she would be relegated, whereas, in her life he would be a 'Peri-Banou', which suggests that, like the Peri of Persian folklore, Dr John is a miraculous being, for whom, if she were to allow her feelings for him to expand, her heart would be a sanctuary for a 'god-like' creature. The difference between the two types of simile used is indicative of their different destinies, and all that Lucy can do is to venerate the being she cannot equal. It does not appear that Charlotte Brontë changed her mind with regard to the delineation of either Dr John or Lucy Snowe. She created a powerful character in Dr John, and an emotionally reticent but extremely sensitive woman in the character of Lucy. At no point in the novel does she alter this point of view.

The rôles of Ginevra Fanshawe and De Hamal are restricted wholly to the second thematic schemata – that portion of the novel concerned with portraying the destinies of the characters. Within that theme, Ginevra's rôle is to show the equable workings of destiny, which mates her with 'a man quite in my way'; furthermore, Ginevra epitomises the values of the fashionable world, and so throws a reflected light of comparison on the more serious Lucy, and finally, she provides the reader with a public view of Lucy's character and appearance. It is certainly an unflattering picture that Ginevra presents, but there is an element of truth in it. She remarks to Lucy that (XIV):

'I suppose you are nobody's daughter, since you took care of little children when you first came to Villette: you have no relations; you can't call yourself young at twenty-three; you have no attractive accomplishments – no beauty. As to admirers, you hardly know what they are: you can't even talk on the subject: you sit dumb when the other teachers quote their conquests. I believe you never were in love, and never will be: you don't know the feeling: and so much the better, for though you might have your own heart broken, no living heart will you ever break. Isn't it all true?'

What Ginevra says is unkind, and it is also dramatically ironic, as she is unaware, as is Lucy at this stage, of the prophetic truth of her statement that 'no living heart will you ever break'. Ginevra also serves to show up the contrast between her destiny and that of Lucy, the difference being established at their first meeting, which takes place on a boat. Ginevra is returning to a school, where she intends to do the minimum amount of work, and extract the maximum amount of pleasure out of life; Lucy, on the other hand, is travelling 'where Fate may lead me', because she has to earn her living. It is fate that directs Lucy to the Pensionnat de Demoiselles, of which Mme Beck is Directrice, and Ginevra a pupil, and destiny, in the person of M. Paul, who decrees that Lucy should be engaged as a governess. The propinquity of place enables Charlotte Brontë to use Ginevra as the observer of Lucy's progress, and her summary, which has already been quoted, agrees with that of Dr John, but diametrically opposes the opinion that M. Paul has of her. Lucy herself sums up the divergent points of view, telling us that (XXVIII):

> You deemed yourself a melancholy sober-sides enough! Miss Fanshawe there regards you as a second Diogenes. M. de Bassompierre, the other day, politely turned the conversation when it ran on the wild gifts of the actress Vashti, because, as he kindly said, 'Miss Snowe looked uncomfortable'. Dr John Bretton knows you only as 'quiet Lucy' – 'a creature inoffensive as a shadow'; he has said, and you have heard him say it: 'Lucy's disadvantages spring from over-gravity in tastes and manner – want of colour in character and costume'. Such are your own and your friends' impressions; and behold! there starts up a little man, differing diametrically from all these, roundly charging you with being too airy and cheery – too volatile and versatile – too flowery and coloury. This harsh little man – this pitiless censor – gathers up all your poor scattered sins of vanity, your luckless chiffon of rose-colour, your small fringe of a wreath, your small scrap of ribbon, your silly bit of lace, and calls you to account for the lot, and for each item. You are well habituated to be passed by as a shadow in Life's sunshine: it is a new thing to see one testily lifting his hand to screen his eyes, because you tease him with an obtrusive ray.

There is also an implied contrast between Ginevra's conduct under adversity, and what we can expect from Lucy after the death of M. Paul, although we are not told more than that she reached old age. Of Ginevra Lucy recalls (XL):

> She had no notion of meeting any distress single-handed. In some shape, from some quarter or other, she was pretty sure to obtain

her will, and so she got on – fighting the battle of life by proxy, and, on the whole, suffering as little as any human being I have ever known.

Thus, Ginevra fulfils a necessary rôle in the novel, as we know that Lucy's future life and conduct will be antithetical to Ginevra's. De Hamal has also a function to perform in *Villette*, apart from his rôle of suitor to Ginevra. He is necessary because, through him, Charlotte Brontë is able to provide a rational explanation for the visitations of the nun. By creating a real nun figure, seen only by Lucy and M. Paul, Charlotte Brontë is able to give a firm foundation to the experience that Lucy and M. Paul share. It is also easier for the reader to distinguish between the literal and figurative meanings that the nun 'person', and the nun 'symbol' represent. The fact that Charlotte Brontë was able to unify the two levels of meaning in one figure, is a indication that she was a great imaginative artist.

It is necessary to quote once more from *Villette*, in order to demonstrate the essential rôle that Mrs Bretton plays in presenting the destiny theme; Lucy comments (XVII):

The difference between her and me might be figured by that between the stately ship cruising safe on smooth seas, with its full complement of crew, a captain gay and brave, and venturous and provident; and the life-boat, which most days of the year lies dry and solitary in an old, dark boat-house, only putting to sea when the billows run high in rough weather, when cloud encounters water, when danger and death divide between them the rule of the great deep. No, the 'Louisa Bretton' never was out of harbour on such a night, and in such a scene: her crew could not conceive it; so the half-drowned life-boatman keeps his own counsel, and spins no yarns.

It will be noticed that the symbols of 'sea' and 'ship', which Charlotte Brontë selected to present the destiny theme, have been consistently used in the portion of the novel concerned with that theme.

During the course of this study of *Villette*, greater emphasis has been given to the discussion of the quality of the language used, because, in this novel, Charlotte Brontë has consistently maintained two levels of expression; the literal, objective, retrospective accounts that Lucy gives us of her life, and the figurative level, in which symbol and metaphor are used for the presentation of the theme. Enough has been said about the subtlety of conception, and the range of meaning of the 'nun' symbol, and of the metaphors of 'ship' and 'sea'. What have not been commented on are the infrequent allusions to 'sunshine', and the prevalence of 'wind and rain' in Lucy's life. These are not used as 'objective correlatives' of states of mind and feeling, as they are in *Jane Eyre,* but are used as a visual and tangible evidence of a Divine Spirit, who has predetermined the destiny of his creatures. As Lucy remarks to Paulina 'it is God's will' that some lives are sunny, whilst 'Other travellers encounter weather fitful and gusty, wild and variable – breast adverse winds, are belated and overtaken by the early closing winter night. Neither can this happen without the sanction of God'. Nature imagery is used, metaphorically and symbolically, to express the actuality of God, his concern about mankind, and the belief that whatever course one's life may take, it is predestined by God. This accords with Charlotte's own ideas, which she expressed to Mrs Gaskell, who relates that (Gaskell: 622):

We talked about the different course through which life ran. She said in her own composed manner, as if she had accepted the theory as a fact, that she believed some were appointed beforehand to sorrow and much disappointment; that it did not fall to the lot of all – as Scripture told us – to have their lines fall in pleasant places; that it was well for those who had rougher paths to perceive that such was God's will concerning them, and to try and moderate their expectations, leaving hope to those of a different doom, and seeking patience and resignation as the virtues they were to cultivate. I took a different view: I thought that human lots were more equal than she imagined; that to some happiness and sorrow came in strong patches of light and shadow (so to speak), while in the lives of others they were pretty equally blended throughout. She smiled, and shook her head, and said she was trying to school herself against ever anticipating any pleasure; that it was better to be brave and submit faithfully; there was some good reason, which we should know in time, why sorrow and disappointment were to be the lot of some on earth. It was better to acknowledge this, and face out the truth in a religious faith.

In conclusion, it can be stated that in *Villette* Charlotte Brontë has created, out of the manifestations of nature, a figurative expression of what her heart felt to be the inner 'Truth' of life. Whatever autobiographical elements from Charlotte Brontë's life there may be in the novel, they have been transformed, so that they are appropriate to the fictional characters that she has created. Realism, of the kind found in *The Professor* and *Shirley,* is entirely absent from the narrative technique used in *Villette.* In fact, one can best describe the novel by quoting from J. S. Mill, who says:

Many of the finest poems are in the form of novels, and in almost all good novels there is true poetry. But there is a radical distinction between the interest felt in a novel as such, and the interest excited by poetry; for the one is derived from *incident,* the other from the representation of *feeling.* In one, the source of the emotion excited is the exhibition of a state or states of human sensitivity; in the other, of a series of states of mere outward circumstances.[4]

In *Villette* the circumstances depicted are merely the centralisation for a cluster of feelings which are engendered by that event, and which are symbolically presented, and thus, in my opinion, *Villette* is an epic poem written in the form of a novel.

6 Conclusion

Beginning with the premise that each novel is an entity in itself, fulfilling certain aims that the author has defined in letters, prefaces or within the novel itself, one can, I think, by a process of empirical analysis, distinguish the predominating elements of narrative pattern used in that work. This form of analysis has been applied independently to each of Charlotte Brontë's novels, and it became clear, in the course of the study, that there were certain narrative techniques peculiar to each work. These narrative techniques constitute the artistic tools of the writer. It now remains necessary to sum up the evidence obtained from the analysis to determine if there is an overall pattern to Charlotte Brontë's style of writing.

In *The Professor* it seems clear that Charlotte Brontë made extensive use of a realistic style, the Preface indicating that her objective was to depict the actions of her protagonist, and the experiences that he encountered on his journey towards economic independence and marriage, without romance or embellishment. However, at crucial periods in William Crimsworth's life, his meeting with Mlle Reuter, and his falling in love with Mlle Frances Henri, the author moves from the depiction of observable experience to the portrayal of her character's thoughts and feelings. For this purpose she drew mainly upon the manifestations of nature to act as visible embodiments of the mood of the character concerned. Furthermore, she employed the artefacts of civilisation, the 'fireside' and the 'garden', as symbols of Crimsworth's progress on the road of life that he has chosen to follow. Thus, apart from the obvious chronological and spatial frame, there is an inner frame of metaphor and symbol, which acts as a further means of structural control, and indicates, by analogy, the progress of the character. None of the artistic devices is complicated or obscure, though they are consistently used throughout the novel.

In *Jane Eyre* it was proved that Charlotte Brontë was concerned with depicting the major experiences of her heroine's life, those which formed her character, and those which will guide her future actions. To portray not only the external events which Jane encounters, but also to know how these affect her mind, spirit and heart, Charlotte Brontë has again utilised manifestations of nature as 'objective correlatives' of subjective states; in particular, using cloud formations, sun, stars, moon and wind for this purpose. Furthermore, to depict Jane's propensities and personality during her childhood, Charlotte Brontë used artefacts from the arts – books and paintings – as 'objective correlatives' of inward states, until such time as Jane had reached sufficient maturity to recognise in nature the mirror of her own thoughts and feelings. The similes and metaphors that the writer has selected are appropriate to the personality of the character, and they are systematically used throughout the novel. In this respect, the novel is as firmly enclosed within a predetermined and consciously used narrative pattern as is *The Professor,* although it is predominantly concerned with the depiction of the inner growth of personality, rather than the portrayal of character-in-action, and, therefore, to use an analogy from painting, the imagery is impressionistic.

Shirley differs from the other two novels in that the structure is based on themes rather than personalities. It is a chronicle of a certain period of history, and portrays certain socio-political themes, the author acting as the observer and narrator of the events. A different tonal quality is to be observed in this novel, in that the author frequently presents the actions of her characters ironically or satirically. There is a limited use of figurative language, and it is isolated from the predominating narrative form by the artificial device of presenting these passages as diary entries. Charlotte Brontë again uses literature as 'objective correlatives' of subjective states, a method she employed in the earlier parts of *Jane Eyre*. However, in *Shirley* this method is more widely applied, and represents the innate tendencies of the total personality, and not only transitory states of thoughts and feelings.

Finally, in *Villette,* Charlotte Brontë has again used a thematic basis for the structure of the novel, as she had previously employed for *Shirley*. Within that frame she has made extensive use of a symbol of a religious connotation to express, by means of an analogue, Lucy Snowe's complex thoughts and feelings about love. Nature imagery is used again in this novel as an 'objective correlative' of states of being, in the sense of that person's unalterable destiny, rather than as the visible embodiment of transitory states of thought and feeling. It has, therefore, a more complex function in *Villette,* as Charlotte Brontë's purpose is to express her belief that human destiny is predetermined. Thus, in comparison with either *The Professor* or *Jane Eyre,* it can be said that the nature imagery in Charlotte Brontë's final completed novel goes beyond the recognisable experiential events of human existence, and is used as an expression of the eternal pattern of the universe as it affects human beings.

The melodramatic elements, which have prejudiced judgement on Charlotte Brontë's novels, have been found to be a truthful description of the normal in *Jane Eyre,* and are both realistic, in the sense of a consciously assumed disguise by De Hamal, and symbolic of Lucy Snowe's and M. Paul's sexual inhibitions and religious uncertainties, in *Villette*. It is also true to say that the use of 'melodrama' is more complex in *Villette* than in the earlier novel, *Jane Eyre,* because the 'nun' figure is used both literally and figuratively, but that in both *Jane Eyre* and *Villette* the melodramatic elements are intrinsic to the structure; they are essential for the delineation of character, and for the working out of the plot. It has also been proved that, whatever autobiographical material Charlotte Brontë might have included in her novels, this is so transformed that it becomes the essence of the experience of the fictional character, as the analysis of the hypochondriacal experience of Crimsworth has shown, or the importance of Dr John's letters to the lonely Lucy Snowe.

From these facts one can conclude that Charlotte Brontë was primarily concerned with the depiction of subjective aspects of human experience, and for this purpose she used Nature both literally and figuratively; to present the unalterable aspects of the universe as manifested in observable Nature, and to show metaphorically the universal pattern of life as it is intuitively perceived by a human being through natural phenomena, which is a particularly Romantic belief, and which is also followed by Wordsworth in his poetry. Charlotte Brontë was aware of the formative and educative influence of Nature on human beings, as she explains in a letter to George Smith (Gaskell: 532):

> If I had never seen a printed volume, Nature would have offered my perceptions a varying picture of a continuous narrative, which, without any other teacher than herself, would have schooled me to knowledge, unsophisticated but genuine.

A similar attitude is expressed by Wordsworth in his poem 'Lines composed. . . above Tintern Abbey' (11.93-102). In view of this unequivocal statement by the author on the function of Nature as a formative influence on her own sensibilities, the critic is entitled to assume that she will similarly portray this influence upon her fictitious characters, which this study has proved to be the case. This attitude towards Nature has been found to be a distinctive trait amongst Romantic writers by Lilian Furst, who states that:

> ... he invariably apprehends the outer world through the mirror of his ego, as against the objective approach of the Realist. What matters to the Romantic is not what *is* but how it *seems* to him. Hence the profound importance of the imagination as the medium of perception.[1]

Charlotte Brontë's own imaginative powers have been clearly shown in the analysis of the narrative techniques she employed in her novels. That she was also a conscientious and dedicated exponent of the art of writing, the following letter to Williams will confirm. She tells him that:

> The first duty of an author is, I conceive, a faithful allegiance to Truth and Nature; his second, such a conscientious study of Art as shall enable him to interpret eloquently and effectively the oracles delivered by these two great deities. The Bells are very sincere in their worship of Truth, and they hope to apply themselves to the consideration of Art, so as to attain one day the power of speaking the language of conviction in the accents of persuasion. . . .[2]

The 'Nature', to which this quotation refers, is the essence of the human spirit, which has its counterpart in inanimate nature, and they are both finite aspects of the eternal Nature of divine creation. In all four novels Charlotte Brontë showed a 'faithful allegiance to Truth and Nature'; all her novels show her 'conscientious study of Art', and her final novel, *Villette,* is the supreme example of the power of her imagination and the power of her expression, in the quality of the narrative technique she employed.

Notes and References

Chapter 2

1. Wimsatt, W.K., *The Verbal Icon.* (University of Kentucky Press, 1954), pp. 115–16. (Reproduced by permission of the publishers.) The entire chapter contains an interesting discussion on the use of imagery by the Romantics.

Chapter 3

1. Monod, Sylvère, 'Charlotte Brontë and the Thirty "Readers" of *Jane Eyre*'. An English translation of the original article in French is printed in the Norton Critical edition of *Jane Eyre*, p. 487. Mr Monod's argument is that the apostrophes to the 'Reader' are devoted to 'rejecting or correcting our mistaken opinions'.
2. Wise, T.J. and Symington, J.A., *The Brontës: Their Lives, Friendships and Correspondence*, vol II, p. 243. Published in 4 volumes by the Shakespeare Head Press, Oxford, 1932.
3. *Turner in the British Museum: Drawings and Watercolours.* A catalogue of an Exhibition at the Department of Prints and Drawings of the British Museum, 1975, and collated by Andrew Wilton, p. 9. (Quoted by permission of the Trustees of the British Museum.)
4. Langford, T., 'The Three Pictures in *Jane Eyre*', *Victorian Newsletter*, 30 (1966), pp. 47–8. Mr Langford interprets the pictures as an allegory of the three most crucial situations in the novel. Mr R.B. Martin, in *The Accents of Persuasion* and Miss J. Millgate, in an article entitled 'Narrative Distance in *Jane Eyre*', *Modern Language Review*, LXIII (1968), also comment on the art passages as being evidence of Charlotte Brontë's interest in art, but none of the critics sees the dramatic possibilities of paintings to illustrate the past.
5. Benvenuto, R., 'The Child of Nature, The Child of Grace', *Journal of English Literary History*, vol 39 (1972), p. 622. Mr Benvenuto's thesis is that 'Charlotte Brontë approaches the opposition between nature and grace as a partisan of both . . . By drawing the line fairly between them, she sets up the conflict in a way that cannot be resolved. The result is a tension and a discord that I do not think Charlotte Brontë intended'.
6. Lock, J. and Dixon, W.T., *A Man of Sorrow: The Life and Times of the Rev. Patrick Brontë* (London, Nelson, 1968), pp. 110–12. An interesting biography, which gives some details that neither Mrs Gaskell nor Mrs Gérin mention.
7. Romieu, Emilie and Georges, *The Brontë Sisters* (London, Skeffington, 1931), p. 172.
8. Vol III of *The Works of John Ruskin*, edited by E.T. Cook and Alexander Wedderburn (London, George Allen, 1903). *Modern Painters*, vol I, p. 234.
9. Ibid., p. 274.
10. Millgate, Miss J., 'Narrative Distance in *Jane Eyre*: The Relevance of the Pictures', *Modern Language Review*, LXIII, No. 2 (April, 1968), p. 319.

Chapter 4

1. Martin, R.B., *The Accents of Persuasion* (London, Faber & Faber, 1966), p. 138.
2. Briggs, Professor Asa, 'Private and Social Themes in *Shirley*', *BST*, Part 68 of

the Transactions, vol 13 No. 3 (1958), pp. 207–14. (Reproduced by kind permission of the Incorporated Brontë Society.)

3. Holgate, Miss I., 'The Structure of *Shirley*', *BST*, Part 72 of the Transactions, vol 14, No. 2 (1962), p. 19. (Reproduced by kind permission of the Incorporated Brontë Society.)

4. Hinkley, Miss L.L., *The Brontës: Charlotte and Emily* (London, Hammond & Hammond, 1947), p. 215.

5. Korg, J., 'The Problem of Unity in *Shirley*', *Nineteenth-Century Fiction*, vol XII, No. 2, (1957), p. 136.

6. Woodward, E.L., *The Age of Reform: 1815–70* (Oxford, The Clarendon Press, 1954), p. 477.

7. Duthie, Dr E.L., *The Foreign Vision of Charlotte Brontë* (London, Macmillan, 1975), p. 141. (Reproduced by permission).

8. Ibid., p. 40.

9. Frye, N., *Romanticism Reconsidered*, Selected Papers of the English Institute, published by Columbia University Press, (1968), p. 5.

Chapter 5

1. Heilman, Dr R.B., 'Charlotte Brontë's "New" Gothic', an article printed in *From Jane Austen to Joseph Conrad*, edited by R. Rathburn and Martin Steinmann, Jr., (University of Minnesota Press, 1958), p. 123.

2. Kroeber, Karl, *Styles in Fictional Structure, The Art of Jane Austen, Charlotte Brontë, George Eliot*. (Princeton University Press, 1971), p. 92. (Reproduced by permission of the publisher).

3. Colby, R.A., '*Villette* and the Life of the Mind', *PMLA*, vol LXXV(September, 1960), pp. 410 and 412.

4. *J.S. Mill's Essays on Literature and Society*, edited and with Introduction by J.B. Schneewind (Collier Books, New York, 1965), p. 104. (Permission granted by Macmillan Publishing Co., Inc., New York.)

Chapter 6

1. Furst, R.L., *Romanticism in Perspective* (London, Macmillan, 1968), p. 58. (Reproduced by permission of the publisher.)

2. Wise, T.J. and Symington, J.A., *The Brontës: Their Lives, Friendships and Correspondence* (Shakespeare Head Press, 1932), vol II, p. 243.

Select Bibliography

M. Allott, *The Brontës: The Critical Heritage* (London, Routledge and Kegan Paul, 1974).

G. Armour-Craig, 'The Unpoetic Compromise: on the relation between Private Vision and Social Order in nineteenth-century English Fiction', printed in *Society and Self in the Novel*, ed. by Mark Schorer, English Institute Essays (Columbia University Press, 1956).

R. Benvenuto, 'The Child of Nature, The Child of Grace', *Journal of English Literary History*, vol 39 (1972).

M.A. Blom, 'Jane Eyre: Mind as Law unto Itself', *Criticism*, vol 15, No. 4 (Fall, 1973).

C.M. Bowra, *The Romantic Imagination* (Oxford University Press, 1950).

A. Briggs, 'Private and Social Themes in *Shirley*', *Brontë Society Transactions*, Part 68, vol 13, No. 3 (1958).

N.S. Bushell, 'Artistic Economy in *Jane Eyre*', *English Language Notes*, vol v, (1968).

R. Chase, 'The Brontës, or Myth Domesticated', reprinted in *Forms of Modern Fiction: Essays collected in honor of Joseph Warren Beach*, ed. W. van O'Connor, (Minneapolis, University of Minnesota Press, 1948).

R.A. Colby, 'Villette and the Life of the Mind', *Publications of the Modern Language Association of America*, vol LXXV, No. 4 (1960)

W.A. Craik, *The Brontë Novels* (London, Methuen, 1968).

F. Dry, *The Sources of Jane Eyre* (Folcroft Library Edition, 1973). A reprint of the 1938 edition, printed by W. Heffer, Cambridge, England, as vol 2 of the Author Brontë sources.

E.L. Duthie, *The Foreign Vision of Charlotte Brontë* (London, Macmillan, 1975).

T. Eagleton, 'Class, Power and Charlotte Brontë', *Critical Quarterly*, vol 14, No. 3 (Autumn, 1972).

D.H. Erikson, 'Imagery as Structure in *Jane Eyre*', *The Victorian Newsletter*, vol 30 (1966).

I.S. Ewbank, *Their Proper Sphere: A Study of the Brontë Sisters as Early Victorian Novelists* (London, Edward Arnold, 1966).

N. Frye, *Romanticism Reconsidered*. Selected papers from the English Institute, ed. N. Frye (Columbia University Press, 1963).

L. Furst, *Romanticism in Perspective* (London, Macmillan, 1968).

W. Gérin, *Charlotte Brontë: The Evolution of Genius* (Oxford University Press, 1967).

J. Gribble, 'Jane Eyre's Imagination', *Nineteenth-Century Fiction*, No. XXIII (1968/9).

B. Hardy, *The Appropriate Form: An Essay on the Novel* (London, The Athlone Press, 1964).

R.B. Heilman, 'Charlotte Brontë's "New" Gothic', article in *From Jane Austen to Joseph Conrad*, ed. R. Rathburn and Martin Steinmann, Jr. (University of Minnesota Press, 1958).

L. Hinkley, *The Brontës: Charlotte and Emily* (London, Hammond & Hammond, 1947).

N.C. Hoar, 'And My Ending is Despair: *Villette* – Charlotte Brontë's Valediction', *Brontë Society Transactions*, vol 16 (1973).

I. Holgate, 'The Structure of *Shirley*', *Brontë Society Transactions*, Part 72, vol 14, No. 2 (1962).

R.E. Hughes, 'Jane Eyre: The Unbaptised Dionysus', *Nineteenth-Century Fiction*, No. XVIII (March, 1964).

R. Kiely, *The Romantic Novel in England* (Harvard University Press, 1972).

E.A. Knies, *The Art of Charlotte Brontë* (Ohio University Press, 1969).

J. Korg, 'The Problem of Unity in *Shirley*', *Nineteenth-Century Fiction*, No. XII (1957).

K. Kroeber, *Styles in Fictional Structure* (Princeton University Press, 1971).

M. Lane, *The Brontë Story: A Reconsideration of Mrs Gaskell's Life of Charlotte Brontë* (William Heinemann, London, 1953).

L. Langford, 'The Three Pictures in *Jane Eyre*', *Victorian Newsletter*, vol 31 (1967).

C. Lemon, 'The Origins of Ginevra Fanshawe', *Brontë Society Transactions*, vol 16 (1971).

L. Lerner, 'The tremulous homely-faced creature: Charlotte Brontë', *Encounter*, No. 45 (July, 1975).

J. Lock and W.T. Dixon, *A Man of Sorrow: The Life, Letters and Times of the Rev. Patrick Brontë* (London, Nelson, 1965)

A. Mackay, *The Brontës: Fact and Fiction* (London, Service and Paton, 1894).

R.B. Martin, *The Accents of Persuasion* (London, Faber & Faber, 1966).

M.B. McLaughlin, 'Past and Future Mind Scapes', *Victorian Newsletter*, No. 41 (1972).

J.S. Mill, *Mill's Essays on Literature and Society*, ed. J.B. Schneewind (New York, Collier Books, 1965).

J.H. Miller, *The Form of Victorian Fiction* (Indiana, Notre Dame University Press, 1968).

J. Millgate, 'Jane Eyre's Progress', *English Studies*, vol 50 (1969).

J. Millgate, 'Narrative Distance in *Jane Eyre*', *Modern Language Review* LXIII (1968).

S. Monod, 'L'Imprécision dans *Jane Eyre*'. Reprinted in the Norton Critical edition of *Jane Eyre*, ed. R.J. Dunn (New York, W. W. Norton, 1971).

R. Offor, *The Brontës: Their Relation to the History and Politics of their Time.* Reprinted from Publications of the Brontë Society (1973).

J. Oldfield, 'The Homely Web of Truth: Dress as a Mirror of Personality in *Jane Eyre* and *Villette*', *Brontë Society Transactions*, vol 16 (1973).

M. Peters, *Charlotte Brontë: Styles in the Novels* (University of Wisconsin, 1973).

J. Prescott, '*Jane Eyre*: A Romantic Exemplum with a Difference', article published in *Twelve Original Essays on Great Novelists*, ed. Charles Shapiro (Detroit, Wayne State University Press, 1960).

E. and G. Romieu, *The Brontë Sisters* (London, Skaffington, 1931).

J. Ruskin, vol III of the *Works of John Ruskin*, ed. E.T. Cook and Alexander Wedderburn (London, George Allen, 1903). *Modern Painters*, vol I.

M.H. Scargill, 'All Passion Spent: A Revaluation of *Jane Eyre*', *University of Toronto Quarterly*, No. 19 (1950).

M. Schorer, *The World We Imagine* (London, Chatto and Windus, 1970).

R. Schorer and R. Kellog, *The Nature of Narrative* (New York, Oxford University Press, 1966).

E.F. Shannon, Jr., 'The Present Tense in *Jane Eyre*', *Nineteenth-Century Fiction*, No. X (September, 1955).

A. Shapiro, 'In Defence of Jane Eyre', *Studies in English Literature*, No. 8 (1968).

C.K. Shorter, *The Brontës and their Circle* (London, J.M. Dent, 1914).

R. Stang, *The Theory of the Novel in England (1850–70)* (London, Routledge & Kegan Paul, 1959).

J. Stevens, 'A Sermon in Every Vignette', *Turnbull Library Record, 1968.* (Wellington, New Zealand).

K. Tillotson, *Novels of the Eighteen-forties* (Oxford University Press, 1954).

J.R. Watson, *The Picturesque Landscape and English Romantic Poetry* (London, Hutchinson, 1970).

I. Watt, 'The Victorian Novel', in *Modern Essays in Criticism* (Oxford University Press, 1971).

W.K. Wimsatt, *The Verbal Icon* (University of Kentucky Press, 1954).

T.J. Winnifrith, *The Brontës and their Background* (London, Macmillan, 1973).

T.J. Wise and J.A. Symington, *The Brontës: Their Lives, Friendships and Correspondence*, in 4 vols (Shakespeare Head Press, Oxford, 1932).

E.L. Woodward, *The Age of Reform: 1815–70* (Oxford, The Clarendon Press, 1954).

Index